NARRATIVE AS TOPIC
AND METHOD
IN SOCIAL RESEARCH

Donileen R. Loseke

University of South Florida

Los Angeles | London | New Delhi
Singapore | Washington DC | Melbourne

QUALITATIVE RESEARCH METHODS SERIES

Series Editor: David L. Morgan, *Portland State University*

The **Qualitative Research Methods Series** currently consists of 60 volumes that address essential aspects of using qualitative methods across social and behavioral sciences. These widely used books provide valuable resources for a broad range of scholars, researchers, teachers, students, and community-based researchers.

The series publishes volumes that:

- Address topics of current interest to the field of qualitative research.

- Provide practical guidance and assistance with collecting and analyzing qualitative data.

- Highlight essential issues in qualitative research, including strategies to address those issues.

- Add new voices to the field of qualitative research.

A key characteristic of the *Qualitative Research Methods Series* is an emphasis on both a "*why*" and a "*how-to*" perspective, so that readers will understand the purposes and motivations behind a method, as well as the practical and technical aspects of using that method. These relatively short and inexpensive books rely on a cross-disciplinary approach, and they typically include examples from practice; tables, boxes, and figures; discussion questions; application activities; and further reading sources.

New and forthcoming volumes in the Series include:

Introduction to Cognitive Ethnography and Systematic Field Work
G. Mark Schoepfle

Narrative as Topic and Method in Social Research
Donileen R. Loseke

Crafting Qualitative Research Questions: A Prequel to Design
Elizabeth (Betsy) A. Baker

Photovoice for Social Justice: Visual Representation in Action
Jean M. Breny and Shannon L. McMorrow

Qualitative Instrument Design: A Guide for the Novice Researcher
Felice D. Billups

How to Write a Phenomenological Dissertation
Katarzyna Peoples

Reflexive Narrative: Self-Inquiry Towards Self-Realization and Its Performance
Christopher Johns

Hybrid Ethnography: Online, Offline, and In Between
Liz Przybylski

For information on how to submit a proposal for the Series, please contact:

- David L. Morgan, Series Editor: morgand@pdx.edu
- Leah Fargotstein, Senior Acquisitions Editor, SAGE: leah.fargotstein@sagepub.com

FOR INFORMATION:

SAGE Publications, Inc.
2455 Teller Road
Thousand Oaks, California 91320
E-mail: order@sagepub.com

SAGE Publications Ltd.
1 Oliver's Yard
55 City Road
London, EC1Y 1SP
United Kingdom

SAGE Publications India Pvt. Ltd.
B 1/I 1 Mohan Cooperative Industrial Area
Mathura Road, New Delhi 110 044
India

SAGE Publications Asia-Pacific Pte. Ltd.
18 Cross Street #10-10/11/12
China Square Central
Singapore 048423

Printed in the United States of America

Library of Congress Cataloging-in-Publication Data

Names: Loseke, Donileen R., author.

Title: Narrative as topic and method in social research / Donileen R. Loseke, University of South Florida.

Identifiers: LCCN 2021035528 | ISBN 9781071851661 (paperback) | ISBN 9781071851692 (adobe pdf) | ISBN 9781071851678 (epub) | ISBN 9781071851685 (epub)

Subjects: LCSH: Narrative inquiry (Research method) | Social sciences—Research.

Classification: LCC H61.295 .L66 2021 | DDC 300.72/3—dc23

LC record available at https://lccn.loc.gov/2021035528

This book is printed on acid-free paper.

Acquisitions Editor: Helen Salmon
Product Associate: Kenzie Offley
Production Editor: Vijayakumar
Copy Editor: Christobel Colleen Hopman
Typesetter: TNQ Technologies
Proofreader: Benny Willy Stephen
Indexer: TNQ Technologies
Cover Designer: Candice Harmon
Marketing Manager: Victoria Velasquez

21 22 23 24 25 10 9 8 7 6 5 4 3 2 1

CONTENTS

PART II • NARRATIVE AS RESEARCH METHOD

PART III • NARRATIVE AS RESEARCH PRACTICE

ACKNOWLEDGMENTS

S AGE and the author are grateful for feedback from Series Editor David L. Morgan, Portland State University, and reviewer Jason R. Jolicoeur, Southeast Community College, during the development of this text.

I would like to thank my students whose questions about narrative research are the reason I wrote this book. I also would like to thank Norm Denizin who, many years ago, told me I needed to get serious about defining research methodology. Although our methodological paths have diverged, I am grateful for his encouragement. Finally, and as is typical, the people at SAGE are a joy to work with.

ABOUT THE AUTHOR

Donileen R. Loseke is a Professor Emeritus in the Department of Sociology at the University of South Florida. She received her BA and MA in psychology (California State University, Dominguez Hills) and her PhD in sociology (University of California, Santa Barbara). Her books include *Narrative Productions of Meanings: Exploring the Work of Stories in Social Life*; *Methodological Thinking: Basic Principles of Social Research Design*, 1st and 2nd edition; *The Battered Woman and Shelters*, which won the Charles Horton Cooley Award from the Society for the Study of Symbolic Interaction; and *Thinking About Social Problems*. She also is the editor of *Current Controversies on Family Violence* (with Richard Gelles) and *Social Problems: Constructionist Readings* (with Joel Best). Numerous journal articles and book chapters report the findings of her empirical research projects, which have been on a variety of topics including evaluation research, social problems, criminal justice, social service provision, occupations, emotion, identity, and narrative and have used a variety of data generation techniques including field experiment, written survey, in-depth interview, ethnography, and document analysis. Among her editorial positions include former editor of the *Journal of Contemporary Ethnography*, advisory editor for *Social Problems*, and deputy editor for *Social Psychology Quarterly*. She received the Mead Lifetime Achievement Award from the Society for the Study of Symbolic Interaction and is the Past-President of the Study of Social Problems as well as Past-President of the Society for the Study of Symbolic Interaction.

INTRODUCTION

Ancient philosophers, including Plato and Aristotle, talked about the importance of narratives—a term interchangeable with what we call "stories" in daily life; narratives have been examined by literary critics and scholars of religion for centuries. Yet, until the 1980s, social scientists all but ignored questions about the work of stories in social life because of perceived irreconcilable differences between what then were understood as the methods and purposes of social research and the characteristics of stories: Social research was about *reducing* complexity while stories are useful precisely because they *emphasize* complexity; social research was about the *objective* world of facts while stories are about the *subjective* world of experiential, emotional, and moral meaning. Transforming stories into an object of social science attention required changing images of both social research and stories.

There were many reasons why the 1980s brought transformations in perceptions of social research. The most central of these are consequences of multiple social changes from globalization, urbanization, mass migration, loss of faith in traditional institutions, and moral fragmentation. These changes raised new questions, particularly about the sources and consequences of deep disagreements: How does the world work and how should it work? What is fact and what is not fact? What is right and what is wrong? The traditional interests and methods of social research were not especially suited to examining questions surrounding the problems of *meaning* that became increasingly essential in understanding the troubles and workings of social organization and social order.

Profound social changes and perceived problems with traditional social research practices combined in the 1980s to produce what is now called the "narrative turn," the increasing interest of professionals inside and outside academia in understanding the centrality of stories in the activities and processes of meaning-making. Observers now maintain that, in multiple ways, stories are a critical—perhaps the most critical—resource in the current world for making sense of self and others; stories that appeal to both hearts and minds are a fundamental component of social change; stories persuade citizens to vote in one way or another, to support or oppose particular government actions and policies, to purchase one or another consumer product. Stories told in social policy hearings shape perceptions of problems and their solutions; stories inform the organization and provision of social services of all varieties; legal proceedings are the telling and evaluating of stories told by prosecutors, defendants, and witnesses. The narrative turn reflects the recognition that stories are everywhere and do important work on all stages of social life from the micropsychological to the macropolitical.

For many theoretical and practical reasons, narrative frameworks now are pervasive throughout the social sciences including in sociology, communication, cultural studies, political science, and gender studies, as well as in the professions of medicine, law, education, and social work. Interest in narrative throughout academic disciplines and professions makes sense because *everything* about narrative is *social*. Narratives are social in their *contents* because, in order for a story to be understandable to more than its author, its contents must reflect understandings about the world relatively shared with others. Narratives are social in their *evaluations* because audiences judge story importance and believability through their practical experiences, common sense, and understandings of how the world works and of how the world should work. Narratives are social in their *consequences* because the meaning-making work they do in sensemaking, persuading, and justifying leads to multiple practical and political consequences for individuals, interactions, organizations, institutions, and culture.

The popularity of narrative *research* is encouraged by the wide variety of questions that can be empirically examined: Questions about narrative content, use, social processes, and consequences can be driven by theory as well as by practical concerns; questions can span academic and professional worlds as well as academic disciplines; questions can transcend common academic divisions of social life into "micro," "meso," and "macro" realms as well as typical academic distinctions between thinking, feeling, and moral evaluation.

Against the acknowledged importance of understanding the work of stories on all stages of social life, narrative research is plagued by three, interrelated problems. The first is quite common in *all* forms of social research which too often proceeds without sufficient attention either to epistemology which makes a research project logically sensible or to methodology which justifies why particular data analytic procedures are appropriate. Insufficient grounding is consequential because it can lead to findings that are too easily dismissed due to basic incompatibility among study questions, data, analytic techniques, and interpretations.

A second problem of narrative research stems from its relative newness and multidisciplinary nature. Simply stated, it is not possible to define "a" literature on narrative because academic works most often are segregated by discipline and, within discipline, further separated by type of question, theoretical perspective, and/or methodological techniques. In consequence, similar concepts can go by different names; concepts can be located within different theoretical frameworks which lead similar terms to have different meanings. When combined, such characteristics produce distinct communities of researchers who share neither common vocabularies nor conceptual frames although they are mutually interested in understanding the characteristics and uses of stories in social life.

A third problem of narrative research is that it is common for manuscripts with narrative in the title or as a keyword to be about something other than narrative. Literature reviews in such cases situate the primary interest within substantive topics; arguments are developed and findings are presented in terms of these substantive topics; discussions center on what data add to knowledge about these particular topics rather than how they increase understandings of the characteristics and work of stories in social life. For this reason, it often seems that "narrative research" is simply a trendy substitution for the traditional term, "qualitative research." As such, the narrative form itself remains theoretically and empirically underexamined, which is unfortunate given the importance of stories in social life.

Against this backdrop of the social importance of stories and the problems of research about stories, my goal is twofold. First, I want to encourage students, scholars, and practitioners across a range of academic disciplines and professional fields to do research on *topics* of narrative, particularly on questions about narrative productions of meaning. Second, I want to develop some fundamentals of research *methods* suitable for designing and implementing such research.

This book is organized in three parts. Part I, Narrative as Research Topic, contains two chapters: Chapter 1 develops a conceptual framework for treating narrative as a research topic; Chapter 2 defines the kinds of questions about narrative that can be explored through empirical research. Part II, Narrative as Research Method, attends to a range of issues surrounding research design and implementation when data are stories and questions are about meaning; Chapter 3 focuses on the epistemological foundation of such research and on the multiple practical issues raised when research questions are about meaning; Chapter 4 is about the practicalities of designing and implementing narrative research. Part III turns to empirical examples of how such research actually is done. Each of Chapters 5–7 uses a small amount of data to examine the analytic tasks of designing research questions, finding appropriate data, sampling decisions, contextualization, data categorization, and communicating study findings.

Although my discussion can apply to narrative research across a wide range of academic and professional areas, my focus is limited in several ways. First, although stories have been a long-standing object of interest to philosophers, literary critics, and religious scholars, I will attend only to narrative research as it is useful in the academic social sciences and in professions such as law, social work, medicine, and education. This directs attention primarily to stories told as "true" rather than as fiction; to stories containing characters who are human, rather than animal or mythical, as well as to stories circulating in the social world rather than residing on kindles or in libraries. By literary standards, the stories that do the most work in social life tend to be poorly written; they rarely are finished but rather are in a constant process of revision; authors can be multiple, unknown, and often unknowable.

Second, I will not cover sociolinguistic approaches to narrative analysis. While such perspectives yield important insights about the *universal* structures of stories, much social research is more interested in examining stories in their historical, political, and cultural *contexts*. Emphasizing the importance of contexts rather than universal structures encourages attention to personal, interactional, organizational, institutional, and political uses and consequences of stories and storytelling.

Third, while some questions about narrative are quite compatible with research frames that are naturalist in epistemology, positivist, postpositivist, or critical in theory, and quantitative in methodology, I will be developing a frame that is *constructionist* in epistemology, *interpretive* in theory, and *qualitative* in method. I do so because such a philosophical, theoretical, and methodological scaffolding is the most capable of empirically exploring questions about narrative constructions of meaning.

Finally, my own experiences as a researcher, teacher, mentor, journal editor, and manuscript reviewer influence both *what* I will discuss and *how* I will discuss it. Simply stated, my experiences have led me to believe that much research about narrative is designed and implemented in ways allowing audiences to challenge the soundness of the research which leads to trivializing the importance of research findings. The most common underlying reason for this is that researchers attempt to examine narrative productions of meaning with methodological tools that are not capable of examining such questions. For this reason, I will focus more attention than is typical on questions of "why" narrative research most productively is shaped in some ways and not others before continuing to demonstrate some of the practical techniques of "how" to do this research.

In brief, I believe that narrative research is important for myriad theoretical and practical reasons, yet in order to achieve its promise researchers must be mindful of every stage of the research process. To this end I hope to offer readers frameworks for thinking about designing and implementing research in ways leading audiences to evaluate the research as sound and the findings as credible and important.

***

Part I begins this process by developing an outline of the field called "narrative," and the kinds of questions about narrative that can be the topic of social research.

PART

I

NARRATIVE
AS RESEARCH
TOPIC

1 CONCEPTUALIZING NARRATIVE FOR SOCIAL RESEARCH

There are multiple understandings of what narratives are and what they do, which is not surprising given the prevalence of interest in narrative across a variety of professions and academic disciplines. While this diversity is beneficial because it offers multiple lens from which to understand the work of stories in social life, it simultaneously can create confusions when similar terms have multiple meanings, when similar meanings go by different names. Hence, I will start by developing a theoretical scaffolding to draw upon in subsequent chapters focusing on narrative as a topic and method of empirical research.[1] This conceptual framework includes narrative characteristics (narrative content, narrative types), narrative authors and audiences, narrative as a sensemaking communication form, and narrative evaluation. It also includes two broad topics surrounding narrative contexts: relationships between narratives and culture which places stories within their social contexts, and relationships between narratives and power which places stories within their political contexts. What unites this diverse list of topics is, in isolation and in combination, each leads to specific empirical questions (Chapter 2), best examined through particular kinds of data and analytic techniques (Part II).

NARRATIVE CHARACTERISTICS

Stories vary remarkably. They can be as short as a sentence or as long as a multiyear television program; they can be told as fact or as fiction, in poetry or in prose; they can be written, spoken, sung, drawn, acted, or danced; they can encourage audiences to think and/or to feel in particular ways.

Narrative Content

Despite remarkable variation, stories are a recognizable form of communication: somewhere (scene) something happens (events) to someone/something (characters).

Story events unfold within *scenes*, the most important of which for social research are physical (such as urban/rural location) and social (such as ideological, historical, cultural, economic). Many common research questions are explicitly about story scenes. Questions about the experiences of immigration, for example, are about consequences of moving from one physical/social scene to another; questions about globalization, urbanization, gentrification, and so on are about the social consequences of changing scenes, and so on. Yet even when not a specific research question, scenes *always* are important because they are a critical *context* for story content, story making, storytelling, and story evaluating. Particular kinds of stories can be told—or cannot be told—in particular times and particular places to particular audiences by particular people for particular purposes. Stories will receive different kinds of audience evaluations depending upon where, when, why, by whom, and to whom they are told.

Second, stories contain *events* which have four characteristics: (1) With the exception of mysteries which contain unrelated events included in order to confuse, most stories contain primarily those events needed to create the story; (2) story events are coordinated by a plot which links events into a coherent whole; (3) regardless of the order in which events are told, events in a completed story are time-ordered which conveys images of causality; (4) events achieve their meaning through *contextualization* within the story. The event of a "woman putting on makeup," for example, has very different meanings depending upon whether the woman is covering bruises from a beating, a sex worker preparing for work, or a happy bride dressing for her wedding.

Third, stories of particular interest to social researchers most often contain *characters*, and these characters are human rather than animal or mythical. There are two broad types of narrative characters. Some stories, especially those told in daily life, contain characters who are unique and embodied, such as stories about "my cousin, Mary" or "the man sitting next to me on the train this morning." Many other stories, especially those told on public stages, contain characters who are disembodied *categories* of people such as "African American," "elderly," "college student," and so on. Additionally, it is common for story characters of both types to be recognizable character *types* such as the "good American," the "fool," the "do-gooder," or the "drama queen." The character types of "victim," "villain," and "hero" are staples in stories associated with social problems, politics, and social protest.[2]

Individual stories vary greatly in the extent to which they are centered on scene, events, or characters, and any story can be told in multiple ways. A story about a "murder," for example, can focus on characteristics of the physical/social/cultural environment surrounding the murder (scene focused); on "what happened" (event focused); or on particular people such as victims, villains, or witnesses (character focused). Story authors decide how to contextualize story events and characters, what to emphasize, what to merely include, and what to exclude. Decisions about contextualization, inclusions, and exclusions are neither random nor inconsequential.

Narrative Types

It sometimes is useful to think of stories in terms of *genre*, a term for stories sharing particular content. Such stories also can be called *formula stories* because they feature predictable plots and characters. While some social observers examine stories in terms of traditional fictional genre classifications such as comedy, tragedy, and drama, other genre classifications pertain particularly to stories circulating in social life including the genres of *social problems* (a plot of devastating harm experienced by characters who are moral people not responsible for the harm they experience), *American Dream* (characters who are moral people working diligently with an expected story outcome of financial and social success), or *coming out* (the experiences of LGBTQ characters who inform family/friends of their sexuality).[3]

Story genre also can focus on story authors. Such genres include *self-stories* which feature the author as the primary character and the author's personal experiences as the primary events. In contrast, *organizational narratives* are authored by organizational workers and administrators and focus on characters taken as instances of typical organizational clients, be they prisoners or patients, students or sociopaths. *Institutional* narratives are authored primarily within policy hearings (government, business, legal) by policy makers and by those who testify. These stories offer images of the problem to be resolved by policy as well as of the categories of people and the types of events policy targets. Finally, *cultural* narratives are stories circulating throughout social life. As with organizational and institutional narratives, cultural narratives primarily feature disembodied characters who are *types* of people in *types* of situations with *types* of experiences. Yet unlike organizational and institutional narratives authored by particular categories of people, cultural narratives often have multiple authors who may or may not be working together to author a story; authors may be unknown. Also, unlike organizational and institutional narratives authored and told in particular sites, cultural narratives circulate on all stages of social life—they are found in media, textbooks, advertisements, speeches, popular culture, social advocacy documents, and so on.

Although it is possible to *analytically* distinguish among narratives on different stages of social life, in practice, stories are *reflexive*: The characteristics of stories produced on any one stage of social life simultaneously are influenced by as well as influence the characteristics of stories produced on other stages.[4]

NARRATIVE MEANING-MAKING

Narrative is a *meaning-making* communication form. This ability to create meaning is increasingly important in a world where meaning is neither fixed nor supported by historical or institutional structures, where there is little agreement about what is right and what is wrong, about how the world works, and about how it should work. Stories within such a world can create three kinds of meanings: Stories create *cognitive* meanings when plots link events into sequences that can be evaluated as meaningful; stories create *emotional* meanings when characters/events encourage emotional reactions; stories create *moral* meanings when characters/events encourage thinking/feeling about what is right and what is wrong. In consequence, narrative is a particularly powerful communication form because it has the ability to appeal *simultaneously* to thinking, feeling, and moral evaluation.[5]

The meaning-making potentials of stories are important throughout social life. How is it possible, for example, to create and maintain a relatively stable sense of self? Many observers argue that this is very difficult in the current era where rapid and constant change, disagreements, and a lack of institutional or community support can lead to an instability in self-understandings. A primary way to achieve an adequate sense of personal identity is through authoring *self-stories* which are stories centering on the author and the author's experiences. Such stories construct meaning from what otherwise might seem random, meaningless experiences; such stories can string together past, present, and anticipated futures into a coherent, meaningful whole.[6]

Or, how is it possible to know how to think, feel, and act toward people, objects, and events that are not known through personal experience? The less possible it is to base cognitive, emotional, moral, and behavioral reactions on practical experience, the more there is no choice but to understand the world around us as instances of *categories* of people, objects, and events. Images of the contents of these categories typically come from stories encountered throughout life. Understandings of story characters and plots can be tools to make sense of encounters and experiences in a complex, constantly changing world filled with strangers.

Stories therefore are a meaning-making communication form that can be used to make sense of self and the surrounding world. This *meaning-making* capability of stories has many other uses: Teachers from preschool to college know that knowledge packaged in story form is an effective way to teach; cognitive researchers find that information in storied form is more easily retained than information in other forms; religious leaders know that stories best convey complex moral lessons. Narratives also can create *justifications*: Stories justify why people in particular social categories are accorded specific levels of moral worth, why public resources are spent in one way rather than another. Still further, with their potentials to create cognitive, emotional, and moral meanings, stories are a basic tool of *persuasion* across the social landscape including in civic life, government, law, medicine, and business.[7] Social activists, for example, typically create stories as ways to convince publics that a condition is at hand causing such intolerable harm that public resources are necessary to eliminate it; public health workers use stories to persuade publics to engage in—or refrain from—particular behaviors; lawyers rely on stories to persuade juries that clients are innocent or guilty.[8]

It is not surprising that observers throughout the social sciences and in a variety of professions are interested in understanding narrative as a communication form because stories do important work on all stages of social life. What work stories do and how stories do this work are questions for social research.

NARRATIVE AUTHORS AND AUDIENCES

Stories require two categories of people: First, there are those who author stories, either as individuals or as organizational agents (politicians, activists, advertisers, lawyers, journalists, social service agency workers, and so on). At times, knowing aspects of authors' positionality can be useful information for understanding story content and story purpose. Yet socially circulating stories often have multiple authors; stories circulating in public life can be changed with each retelling; authors can be disguised or invisible; authors can occupy multiple, often conflicting positionalities. For such reasons, relationships between story content and story authors are best understood as empirical questions rather than as unexamined assumptions.

Stories also need an *audience*, people who encounter (hear, see, read) and evaluate them. This might be an internal audience of the self; it might be a limited number of specific others such as friends or family, a specific category of person (such as readers of a particular blog or voters in a particular district), or an unspecified generic (the public, Americans). Questions about audiences can be quite complicated in the current era where diversity in audiences means that story characteristics praised by some will be condemned by others. Further, socially important stories in the current era can have two audiences: The audience for whom the story was intended, and the audience encountering a story as relayed (and sometimes repeatedly modified) through media in its many varieties.[9]

NARRATIVE EVALUATION

Many stories authored and encountered in daily life are insignificant. They are about trivial events; they are told once or twice to family, coworkers, or friends, and then forgotten. What distinguishes such inconsequential stories from those that go on to shape social movements or public policy, that become widely accepted justifications for war or for peace, for harsh or accepting treatment of immigrants? This question is about the characteristics of *good stories* which I will define as stories with *potentials* to be evaluated as believable and important by relatively large audiences and therefore with *potentials* to become resources for meaning-making based on thinking, feeling, and/or moral evaluation.

Story evaluation is influenced by story *performance*: How, where, and by whom is the story told? Socially circulating ideas about who has the right to tell stories and about whose stories should be believed necessarily influence story evaluation. A good story is one evaluated as told by an appropriate person in an appropriate manner, in an appropriate place, to an appropriate audience.[10]

I will focus on evaluations of story *content*. Obviously, a good story is evaluated by audiences as *interesting* and *important* simply because stories evaluated as not interesting or as not important will be ignored. A story reaching a threshold of perceived interest and importance has the potential for becoming a good story if it is evaluated as *believable*, as judged through comparing perceived story contents to practical experience, common sense, and understandings of morality.[11]

Critically, a story is evaluated as *true* to the extent that it is believable, and it is believable to the extent that it is evaluated as relatively conforming to common sense, practical experiences, and moral evaluations. Story truth therefore is experiential, emotional, and moral. What is absolutely essential in narrative research is accepting what we all know from practical experience: There is *no necessary relationship* between story truth and truth as objectively measured or as grounded in the evaluations of officially certified "experts." The ways in which stories achieve evaluations of believability is an empirical question.

NARRATIVE AND CULTURE

Any question about stories can be examined or understood only by placing story making, storytelling, and story evaluating within culture. While "culture" can be defined in many ways, I will define it as *systems of meanings* that can be used by social actors to accomplish practical agendas, including those of meaning-making in its many varieties for its many purposes.[12]

Cultural systems of meaning are of two types. Those organizing ways of thinking are *symbolic codes*,[13] densely packed systems of ideas about how the world works, how the world should work, and of expected rights and relationships among people. Symbolic codes therefore are both statements of assumed fact (how the world does work, how people do act) and moral evaluations (how the world should work, how people should act). Social life can be conceptualized as dense, interlocking systems of meaning such as individualism, capitalism, family, democracy, the American way of life, victim, villain, citizen, terrorist, and hero.[14]

Cultural systems of meaning also surround emotion. Called *emotion codes*,[15] these meanings are cognitive models of what emotions are expected where, when, and by whom, as well as how emotions should be internally experienced, externally expressed, and morally evaluated. As with symbolic codes, emotion codes are systems of assumptions and expectations both about what is (how people do feel and express feelings) as well as what should be (how people should feel and express feelings).[16]

Systems of meaning shape stories in multiple ways. The social process of *storytelling*, for instance, is surrounded by expectations about where, when, and by whom what kinds of stories must be told, can be told, and cannot be told. This includes ideas about what specific categories of people (such as parents, physicians, judges) have the right to request—or demand—stories, and which categories of people (such as children, patients, defendants) have obligations to tell the stories requested. Culture also is a system of ideas about what stories should be evaluated as truthful (for example, those told by adults or by credentialed professionals) and which can be dismissed (such as stories told by children, prisoners, or by those diagnosed as incompetent).[17] Additionally, culture is a system of ideas about expected story content: Most people know that when a physician asks, "how are you," the request is for a story about health; when a lawyer says "tell us what happened" the request is for a story about the event being evaluated by the court, and so on.

Cultural meaning systems also include ideas about stories that should not or cannot be told. *Unspeakable* stories are those whose plots contain such horror (such as stories of survivors of the Holocaust or Hiroshima bombing) that those who experienced it find it too painful to tell. *Undiscussable* stories are those where a storyteller might wish to tell a story of horror yet find no audience willing to listen. *Incomprehensible* stories are those not reflecting cultural systems of meaning: Stories of "sexual harassment," for example, could not be told until there was a category called "sexual harassment"; such stories could not be taken seriously until sufficient numbers of people were convinced such stories were to be believed rather than assumed to be false.[18]

Culture also shapes story *content* for the obvious reason that stories can be understood by those other than their author only when they incorporate relatively shared systems of meaning. The more a story scene, characters, and plot reflect meaning systems that are widely shared and evaluated as important, the more likely the story will be positively evaluated by more than a few audience members. The more a story contains systems of meaning that are not widely shared and/or that are contentious and subject to disagreement, the more likely the story will not achieve widespread approval.

Cultural meaning systems shape the processes of story making, storytelling, and story evaluating. Yet while culture is central to understanding the work of stories, cultural meaning is *not* deterministic. Meaning systems are what ethnomethodologists refer to as "resources," they are socially circulating images, ideas, norms, values, expectations, and so on that, on a case-by-case basis, people can decide to use, modify, or ignore in order to accomplish practical agendas including those surrounding understanding self and others, as well as political, legal, or social persuasion or justification. Further, culture is fragmented rather than wholistic. Indeed, a characteristic of the current era is the apparent inability of social members to agree on much of anything. There are wide variations in the extent to which any particular meaning system is known, as well as in how particular meanings are morally evaluated by different audience segments. Because particular stories reflect particular meaning systems, it follows that the more diverse the audience, the more likely it is that *any* story will receive evaluations ranging from highly positive to highly negative.

That said, it remains that while culture is neither deterministic nor wholistic, culture is about meanings that are relatively shared and without shared meanings, stories would be understandable only to their authors. The ways in which stories reflect and perpetuate and/or challenge particular cultural meaning systems are topics for empirical investigation.

NARRATIVE AND POWER

Although many academic scholars and other professionals have discovered the importance of stories in social life, it remains that many others have not and continue to believe that narrative does not require (perhaps does not even deserve) scholarly attention because stories are a fanciful, trivial, and insignificant communication form often conveying a less than truthful image of empirical reality as scientifically measured. I would respond by arguing that, regardless of any relationship between story content and scientific truth, the structures and processes of power of *any* type cannot be fully understood without attending to the ways in which socially circulating narratives both reflect and perpetuate power. Narrative is about power; power runs throughout the processes of authoring, telling, and evaluating stories. Story consequences likewise can strengthen or diminish power in its many objective and subjective forms.

Power shapes *storytelling* because cultural meaning systems influence who can—and who cannot—tell what kinds of stories in what kinds of circumstances as well as whose stories likely will be believed and whose likely will be silenced or ignored. Power shapes story *content* because stories with potentials to appeal to the largest audiences will incorporate the systems of meaning shared by those in relatively privileged audience segments although these meanings often are *not* those of the powerless.

Further and critically, the *consequences* of stories are tools of both *subjective* and *objective* power. Socially circulating stories used as models of identity locate individuals in social and moral hierarchies with accompanying constellations of benefits and burdens, rights and responsibilities. Stories shaping public opinion yield public concern—or the lack of concern; public concern influences social policy, social policy confers objective and subjective benefits and burdens on particular population segments. And, organizationally sponsored stories within social service agencies become yardsticks to measure and morally evaluate characteristics of individual people using agency services and this, of course, influences how individual clients are treated and what they likely will—and will not—receive from the organization. Narrative and power are mutually created and mutually sustained.

NARRATIVE AS TOPIC IN SOCIAL RESEARCH

The narrative communication form is important on all stages of social life from the most private and personal to the most global and political. Clearly, stories are not simple "conveyers of information." On the contrary, the narrative communication form is central to the organization and processes of social life and therefore should be a topic of research. My goal in this chapter was to establish a basic vocabulary and conceptual framework amenable to treating narrative, particularly narrative content, as a research topic. While readers will need to consult other works to fill in the details of this most rudimentary frame, it seems sufficient to continue to the topic of social research: What kinds of empirical questions are posed by the presence, contents, uses, and consequences of narratives in social life?

NOTES

1. I do not pretend to offer anything near a complete review of the existing literature which is considerable, ever expanding, and located across multiple disciplines and professions. For general treatments of narrative: Berger (1997), Berger and Quinney (2005), Bruner (1987), Ewick and Silbey (1995), Fisher (1984), Frye (1957), Gubrium and Holstein (2009), Holstein and Gubrium (2000), Loseke (2019), Polletta et al. (2011), Polkinghorne (1988). For narrative in education: Bell (2002), Young (2009); in medicine: Frank (1995); in nursing: Casey, Proudfoot, and Corbally (2016), Green (2013), Wang and Geale (2019); in law: Amsterdam and Bruner (2000), Dinerstein (2007); in public policy: Roe (1994).

2. For the victim character see Holstein and Miller (1990) and Loseke (2003). For the hero character see Bergstrand and Jasper (2018) and Klapp (1954). For the villain character see Brooks (1976) and Singer (2001).

3. Works about narrative genres include the genres of war (Smith 2005), drinking (Sandberg, Tutenges, and Pedersen 2019); social problems (Loseke 2003), romance novels (Radway 1984); nonfictional autobiographies (Gergen 1994); coming out (Klein et al. 2015), talk shows (Squire 2002); American Dream (Rowland and Jones 2007; Samuel 2012).

4. Shuman (2005) offers a compelling analysis of what happens when stories "travel" from the original storyteller to others such as journalists, researchers, and social service providers. When stories travel they can be "repackaged" to exemplify morals never intended by the storyteller.

5. Asserting that people are drawn to communication forms that can appeal simultaneously to thinking, feeling, and moral evaluation goes back to Aristotle (1926, 13–14) and is confirmed in the present day by observers who argue our "cognitive beliefs about how the world is, our moral vision of how the world should be, and our emotional attachment to that world march in close step" (Jasper 1997, 108).

6. See, for example, Becker (1997), Holstein and Gubrium (2000), Linde (1993), and Plummer (1995).

7. Andrews (2019) examines the work stories do to encourage or discourage political forgiveness; Loseke (2009) and Smith (2005) explore how presidents tell stories encouraging publics to define war as morally necessary; see Reich (2005) for the argument that political persuasion is best done through storytelling.

8. Empirical examples of relationships between stories and how social workers understand their clients include Järvinen and Anderson (2009), Emerson (1997), Loseke (2001), Marvasti (2002), and Nolan (2002). For examples of how institutional narratives justify policy see Balch and Balabanova (2011), Barton (2007), Keeton (2015), Stewart (2012). Considerable research demonstrates how stories are the most effective form of public health communication (Frank et al. 2015, McQueen et al. 2011). Observers of social movements have been particularly attuned to the importance of stories to social

movement organization (Davis 2002, Fine 2002), especially to how narratives mobilize both movement participants (Lauby 2016, Powell 2011) and general publics (Burchardt 2016).

9. Most obviously, stories taken out of the context of their telling can radically transform their meaning; there can be wholesale changes in images of narrative plots, characters, and morals as stories are told and retold.

10. Much of this interest in the social processes of storytelling comes from scholars of performance studies. See Alexander (2017) and Polletta et al. (2011) for sociologically centered treatments of narrative performance criteria.

11. As succinctly stated by Joseph Davis, a believable story, "is one that makes sense given what audiences think they know, what they value, what they regard as appropriate and promising" (2002, 17–18).

12. I am drawing from Anne Swidler (1986, 273) who defined culture as "publicly available symbolic forms"; Eviatar Zerubavel's (1996, 428) notion of culture as "impersonal archipelagos of meaning…share[d] in common," and Clifford Geertz (1973, 5) who defined culture as "webs of significance." Culture, in this sense, is systems of meaning that are important because they can be understood as a "tool kit" (Swidler 1986) or a "collection of stuff" (DiMaggio 1997) that social members can use, modify, or ignore in order to make sense of selves, others, and the world around us.

13. What I am calling symbolic codes go by other names including interpretive codes (Cerulo 1998), ideological codes (Smith 1999), and collective representations (Durkheim 1961).

14. There is a considerable literature examining systems of meaning such as those surrounding democracy (Alexander and Smith 1993), individualism (Bellah et al. 1985), American values (Hutcheson et al. 2004), victim (Holstein and Miller 1990, Best 1997), terrorist (Flopp 2002), and villain (Brooks 1976, Loseke 2009, Singer 2001).

15. Stearns and Stearns (1985) call these systems of meaning emotionologies; Gordon (1990) calls them emotional cultures; Hochschild (1979) calls them feeling rules, framing rules, and display rules.

16. The considerable literature unpacking the contents of emotion codes includes the codes of sympathy (Clark 1997), empathy (Ruiz-Junco 2017), jealousy (Stearns 1990), anger (Lambek and Solway 2001), and fear (Altheide 2002).

17. Excellent summaries of culture and storytelling can be found in Ewick and Silbey (1995), Linde (2010), and Polletta et al. (2011).

18. Stein (2009) and Simic (2003) discuss the characteristics of untellable and undiscussable stories.

2

EMPIRICAL QUESTIONS ABOUT NARRATIVE

Although the term "narrative" often is in the titles or keywords of books and articles authored by social researchers, it nonetheless is common for literature reviews, data analysis, and conclusions in these works to focus on substantive topics rather than on narrative. While using narrative to examine substantive topics has yielded many important insights on a wide variety of topics and therefore should be continued, narrative research has done too little to increase understandings of how stories work and the work stories do in social life. My argument is that it is productive to *foreground* questions about the production, use, and consequences of the narrative communication form in social research.

Because empirical research addresses questions about how the world works, each research project begins with a question or an interrelated series of questions. Although questions leading research often are only implicit in published research, it is good practice to have explicit and precise questions when designing, conducting, and reporting research. Explicit questions help keep readers (and researchers themselves) tightly focused on the particular issues at hand and therefore help avoid becoming sidetracked into topics that are tangential.

As a framework for presentation, I will order possible research questions about narrative into five general categories, the first of which is about processes and actors: What are the social processes and who are the social actors involved in story making, storytelling, and story evaluation? While important, I will not dwell on these for the simple reason that questions about the processes and actors involved in authoring, telling, and evaluating stories pose no unique issues for social research and therefore are amendable to exploration via traditional research methodologies outlined in countless existing textbooks.

I will center attention on four other kinds of questions about the characteristics of stories themselves: Story meaning is derived from perceived story content, so what is story content? How are story meanings used in personal, organizational, and institutional spheres of social life? What are the relationships among the meanings of stories produced on different stages of social life? What are the subjective and objective consequences of narrative productions of meaning? Reasons for targeting these questions about the contents, uses, and consequences of narrative meaning are philosophical, theoretical, and methodological: The importance of stories in social life relates to their meaning-making capacities; questions about meaning are philosophical and theoretical; such questions pose a variety of specific methodological issues for social research design and implementation that are not a central component of traditional canons of social research.

While I will include multiple examples of the kinds of questions researchers have asked about narrative, I am not offering an exhaustive catalogue of question types. On the contrary, I hope that readers will find inspiration in the questions asked by others and be led to asking new kinds of questions and empirically pursuing their answers in new types of ways. Further, while I am sorting questions into categories, I do so merely to organize my comments and do *not* offer these categories as a typology. It will be clear that many of the examples I use to demonstrate one type of question easily could be used to demonstrate another; questions asked by researchers often both combine and blur the categories I am using here. Again, I hope this encourages readers to think creatively about how to ask empirical questions about narrative productions of meaning.

QUESTIONS ABOUT SOCIAL PROCESSES AND SOCIAL ACTORS

There are many questions about narrative as the social *processes* of story making, storytelling, and story evaluating which involve different categories of social *actors*—those who author stories, tell them, and evaluate them for their interest, importance, and believability.

Story Authors and Story Making

First are questions about *story authors* and *story making*. For example, our current era is complex and characterized by disagreements of many varieties. This raises questions about stories produced by authors in different social categories:

> *How do the stories told by youths make sense of conflict in their everyday lives and how do their stories compare to media-driven stories of youths as uncontrollable and violent predators?*
>
> (Morrell et al. 2000)

Or by authors with different personal characteristics:

How do jury members with different racial and class characteristics construct racialized stories in death penalty cases?

(Fleury-Steiner 2002)

Questions also can be asked about how stories are created through the coordinated or uncoordinated work of multiple authors:

How were public images of "ethnic identities" formed through stories authored by professional heritage preservers, ethnic leaders, researchers, media, and ethnic organizations?

(Berbrier 2000)

And, there are questions about how *context* influences how authors write stories:

How are the self-stories of clients generated by organizational workers and routines in places such as support groups for abused women, human service agencies, and divorce proceedings?

(Holstein and Gubrium 2000)

Stories are created by people who sometimes act as individuals and sometimes as organizational or institutional actors. Appreciating the work of stories requires understanding the characteristics of story authors and the workings of story making.

Storytellers and Storytelling

While too often ignored by social researchers (Polletta et al. 2011), there are important questions about *storytellers* and *storytelling*. Storytelling, for example, is surrounded by cultural expectations influencing who can—and who cannot—tell stories. This leads to a variety of questions about stories told by people in particular social categories:

How are stories told by African-American women (Collins 1989), or survivors of rape, incest, and sexual assault (Alcoff and Gray 1993) silenced?

Likewise, social contexts determine the expectable or desirable contents of stories that *must* be told:

> *What kinds of stories must be told by asylum seekers wishing to be granted entry to the United States?*
>
> (Bohmer and Shuman 2018)

While the process of storytelling simultaneously is the process of *story distribution*, the current era adds complexity when stories are relayed endlessly through media of many varieties. Questions can be about how media processes shape stories:

> *How did UK press selection and presentation of knowledge construct the narrative of "managed migration" and the counternarrative of "immigration as chaotic and uncontrolled" in debates over access to labor markets for new European Union citizens?*
>
> (Balch and Balabanova 2011)

Or, about how authors work to distribute their own stories:

> *How do members of social policy advocacy groups use twitter to disseminate their preferred stories of nuclear energy?*
>
> (Gupta, Kuhika, and Wehde 2018)

Once authored, stories must be conveyed to audiences. Whether this is in poetry, prose, song, or dance, whether it is in person or through technology, there are multiple empirical questions about how and by whom stories are transmitted to audiences.

Story Audience and Story Evaluating

Story making and storytelling do not matter if there is no *audience*, those who encounter (hear, see, read) stories and evaluate the extent to which they are important and believable. Questions about audience evaluation are particularly significant in the current era characterized by so little agreement about meanings and moral evaluations. While it is a truism that the meanings and evaluations of *any* particular story depend upon characteristics of audiences doing this evaluation, how audiences with particular characteristics evaluate particular stories should *not* be merely assumed and rather should be treated as empirical questions to be investigated:

How do narratives of personal experience among members in a Midwestern comedy club shape their receptibility to the racial discourse in the stories told by standup comedians?

(DeCamp 2017)

How do narrative conventions and institutional imperatives of media produce the meaning of television news on the global level?

(Kavoori 1999)

In conclusion, stories are a social product in that people—as individuals or as organizational actors—within specific historical, cultural, and political contexts decide how to shape story scenes, characters, and events. Likewise, the perceived meanings, importance, and believability of stories is the social product of audience evaluation. Everything about the production, distribution, and evaluation of stories is social and therefore a legitimate and important topic of social research.

QUESTIONS ABOUT NARRATIVE MEANING

Stories are important because they are a meaning-making form of communication. This raises questions about the perceived contents, uses, and consequences of storied meaning.

Story Content

Because meaning is derived from perceived story content, research can focus directly on content. Such questions can be quite straightforward:

How do news articles from the Los Angeles Times about events on the U.S.-Mexican border construct a "Mexican Threat" narrative?

(Aguirre, Rodriguez, and Simmers 2011)

Explicit questions about story content also can attend to how particular cultural systems of meaning (symbolic or emotion codes) are contained in stories:

How does the therapeutic code organize the treatment of personal stories told on the Oprah Winfrey show?

(Illouz 2003)

Additionally, explicit questions about story content can compare the contents of stories produced by different social actors:

> *What are the key themes within and across the narratives of younger and older generations of non-binary people produced on blogs and internet forums?*
>
> (Yeadon-Lee 2016)

> *How do the stories told by perpetrators and non-perpetrators of intimate partner violence demonstrate how violence is incorporated into the cultural narrative of masculinity?*
>
> (James-Hawkins et al. 2019)

Or, they can be about how story content changes over time:

> *How has the narrative of obesity authored by the contemporary, mainstream media changed over time?*
>
> (Shugart 2011)

Story Use

While some research is explicitly centered on questions about story content, it is more common for questions about content to be *implicit* and to underlie other kinds of questions about stories. One of the most central of which is about how, in a world of constant change and profound moral disagreements, stories create meaning at all levels of social life.

Stories and Personal Meaning-Making

A world characterized by constant change and lack of shared meaning makes it difficult to construct and maintain a solid sense of the meaning of self, others, objects, and experiences. There is ample empirical evidence that stories are a primary tool helping individuals to make meaning in such environments. Stories can offer guidelines for how to make sense of newly encountered events and people as well as events and people beyond personal experiences.[1]

American observers have been most interested in exploring how individuals author *self-stories*. These stories featuring the self as the central character and personal experiences as the central plot can create a sense of personal meaning, particularly in times of trouble such as that created by:

Social disapproval from others:

How do drug users author stories about themselves in ways creating symbolic boundaries between them and other users evaluated as morally suspect?

(Copes et al. 2016)

Illness:

How do people with the contested illness of chronic fatigue syndrome construct stories of resistance?

(Sanchez 2020)

Personal trauma:

How do survivors of sexual abuse make and remake the meaning of their experiences over the course of their lives and at different stages of recovery?

(Harvey et al. 2000)

Self-stories also can be used to advance *public* goals:

How do celebrities explicitly present their own stories of health problems as ways to educate, to inspire, and to encourage social activism among the general public?

(Beck et al. 2014)

How do people seeking funding for medical procedures create their self-stories on GoFundMe in ways appealing to the lived experiences and moral assumptions of members of their own social network?

(Paulus and Roberts 2018)

Stories featuring the self as the primary character and experiences of the self as the primary action do a variety of work on both private and public stages of social life. Understanding how these stories are shaped and what purposes they serve are important topics for social research.

Stories and Organizational Meaning-Making

Organizational narratives are authored and used by organizational participants to make sense of the organization and their experiences in it.

Considerable research has focused on social movement actors, such as how they use stories as a recruitment tool:

> *How do social movement organizations use narratives as a key resource for recruiting members and sustaining participation?*
>
> (Powell 2011)

Or, on how social movement actors use stories to make sense of disappointing experiences:

> *How did social activists working on changing Argentina's abortion laws turn to storytelling when their hopeful expectations were disappointed?*
>
> (Borland 2014)

Research also might attend to how stories can be used to frame public images of problems and their solutions:

> *How did undocumented youth activists use storytelling to reframe the debates around immigration reform and position themselves as the rightful leaders of a movement that had been adult citizen dominated?*
>
> (Cabaniss 2019)

Predictably, organizations author and promote dissimilar stories so there are questions about variations in stories authored by different organizations:

> *How do gun rights organizations and gun control organizations portray the victims of gun violence, particularly with respect to the race and age of victims?*
>
> (Merry 2018)

Additionally, stories can encourage alliances among like-minded others which can be a topic of empirical research:

> *How do stories encourage the emergence of informal networks of environmental activists interested in alternative agricultural methods?*
>
> (Ingram, Ingram, and Legano 2014)

Considerable research also demonstrates the importance of organizational narratives in a variety of social service organizations where stories provide workers with models for how to think about the characteristics, problems, and needs of organizational clients which, in turn, can be used to justify organizational services, rules, and methods of service provision. Questions about organizational narratives in social services can be phrased very broadly:

> *How do socially circulating stories about the characteristics of people with substance use problems serve as a resource for welfare workers?*
>
> (Selseng 2017)

Or, they can be very specific:

> *How do nurses' narratives of 'trivial' patients justify guideline-violating gatekeeping to hospital emergency rooms?*
>
> (Johannessen 2014)

Research on stories in social service settings also can examine differences between the characteristics of stories expected by the organization and the stories told by their clients:

> *How do the characteristics of stories necessary to obtain a domestic violence restraining order differ from the characteristics of stories told by women victims seeking such protection?*
>
> (Emerson 1997)

And, research can examine the organizational work of shaping clients' stories into those preferred by the organization:

> *What kinds of stories of disabled children did discussion facilitators elicit and encourage in a support group for parents of disabled children?*
>
> (Barton 2007)

There are multiple questions about the contents and uses of stories written by and for organizational actors. Because these stories do meaning-making work they are an important topic for empirical research.

Stories and Institutional Meaning-Making

Stories can be authored in *institutional* settings such as law, education, medicine, social work, and government. Empirical questions about the meaning-making work of stories in such settings can be about the *content* of stories told in places such as courts and social policy hearings:

> *How do public narratives about teachers within the Norwegian national curriculum documents regulating teacher education construct teacher identities?*
>
> (Søreide 2007)

Questions also can examine narratives and the *process* of policy making:

> *How are narratives developed, codified, revised and diffused in policy debates and policy-making surrounding migration policy?*
>
> (Boswell, Geddes, and Scholten 2011)

Or, questions can center on how stories shape public opinion:

> *How did President George W. Bush manage the immigration issue by promoting stories that simultaneously contained the themes of exclusion and inclusion?*
>
> (Edwards and Herder 2012)

Questions also can be about how the meaning created by stories serves to justify law and social policy:

> *How did policymakers use stories from the Old Testament of the Christian Bible to motivate support for the Indian Removal Act of 1830?*
>
> (Keeton 2015)

> *How do the stories American Presidents tell about the necessity for war create the cultural foundations for justifying policies of war?*
>
> (Smith 2005)

Stories are woven throughout the institutional spheres of social life and do meaning-making work that shapes images of problems and their solutions, encourages particular constellations of public opinion, as well as justifies laws and policies. How stories work and the work stories do in institutional arenas are empirical questions for social research.

Stories and Cultural Meaning-Making

Stories that circulate broadly through media of all varieties, speeches, textbooks, songs, advertising, and so on can be called cultural stories because their pervasiveness shapes meaning at the most broad level of culture. Studies might ask about the contents of such broadly circulating stories:

> *How do stories from American and Japanese school textbooks display cultural values and characteristics?*
>
> (Imada 2012)

Or, studies might ask how cultural stories influence personal experience:

> *How do dominant cultural narratives about race influence the lived experiences of workplace racism and resistance among Black youth and young adults?*
>
> (Hasford 2016)

> *How do dominant cultural narratives about aging complicate the ascription of meaning to later life?*
>
> (Laceulle and Baars 2014)

I will continue discussing the work of cultural narratives in the next section.

QUESTIONS ABOUT REFLEXIVITY OF NARRATIVE MEANINGS

Although it is possible to *analytically* distinguish among narratives authored on different stages of social life, stories in actual use are fully reflexive which means stories told on one stage of social life both influence and are influenced by those told on other stages. Stories, in other words, can migrate from one social space to another and this leads to many important empirical questions.

The most common question about narrative migration is about relationships between stories widely circulating through media, speeches, documents, and so on (cultural narratives) and stories told by individuals. While cultural narratives are resources that can be used by individuals to craft their own stories, research can focus on *differences* between cultural stories and self-stories:

> *What explanatory models of illness do people use to tell stories of their own pain and suffering? How do individual stories differ from the most commonly circulating cultural stories?*
>
> (Garro 1994)

Questions driving research might examine how cultural narratives simultaneously are both accepted *and* challenged in self-stories:

> *How can an influential theory of "boys' anti-school attitudes" be interpreted as a master narrative that is reproduced but also contradicted and subverted by students and teachers in local contexts?*
>
> (Jonsson 2014)

> *How do rural gays and lesbians engage with and modify cultural narratives that link gay and lesbian identities to urban spaces?*
>
> (Kazyak 2011)

Conversely, questions can be problem oriented and centered specifically on perceived *negative* consequences of culturally circulating stories:

> *How do teen moms distance their own stories from prevailing social/ cultural stories about the problems of teen motherhood?*
>
> (Barcelos and Gubrium 2014)

> *How does the cultural story of the meanings and problems of opiate addiction as an incurable condition tend to encourage workers in drug treatment centers to view agency clients as chronic addicts?*
>
> (Järvinen and Andersen 2009)

Or, research can address how individuals use culturally circulating stories in ways leading to *beneficial* results:

> *How do women who were in prison draw from hegemonic cultural characters and storylines in order to resist the stigma associated with a felon identity and refashion and reaffirm their identities by aligning with conventionality?*
>
> (Ospal 2011)

Stories are authored, told, and evaluated on every stage of social life; those authored and told on one stage often migrate to other stages and are used for purposes other than those originally intended. This, of course, leads to multiple questions about the characteristics, uses, and consequences of such narrative migration.

QUESTIONS ABOUT THE CONSEQUENCES OF NARRATIVE MEANING

One central reason why social observers were slow to take up narrative as a topic of study were assumptions from popular reasoning that stories are a frivolous communication form and therefore only of entertainment value and not worthy of scientific attention. Yet given the extensive and ever-growing evidence that stories can have multiple and significant consequences for individuals, organizations, and culture, social researchers do well to explicitly address the question of the ways in which narrative meaning matters to real people in real time. A critical task for scholars of narrative continues to be that of establishing *why* the narrative communication form is worthy of attention. This requires demonstrating subjective and/or material *consequences* of narrative meaning-making.

Meaning Consequences as Research Topic

Understanding meaning consequences can be the *focus* of research. For example, researchers might ask:

How do stories of migrants shape policy debates in Europe?

(Borland 2014)

How do women's understandings of the "romantic narrative" promote their use of condoms for contraception but not for safe sex?

(Kirkman 1998)

How do political disinformation campaigns gain credibility by embedding themselves within central master narratives of national decline and rebirth?

(Levinger 2018)

Questions also might center on how *subjective* processes of meaning creation can lead to *material* consequences:

How do personal testimonies in town hall listening sessions for proposed amendments to the Americans with Disabilities Act reflect and affect the images of "who counts" as disabled and "what counts" as reasonable accommodations?

(Welch 2020)

Because narrative communication forms are pervasive and do so much work at every level of social life, empirical questions about their consequences can be framed more broadly. Researchers, for example, have explored how narrative figures into multiple dimensions of national and international *political conflicts* such as those between the stateless Karen people who have fought for political autonomy and independence from the Burmese government for over a half century:

> *How do future Karen leaders construct stories that deal with the challenges of forming the unity and legitimacy of a Karen identity?*
>
> (Kuroiwa and Verkuyten 2008)

Indeed, researchers might ask about relationships between narrative and the very *structure of social life*:

> *What do autobiographical stories of "awakenings" (such as religious conversion, embracing a new sexual orientation, recovered memories of childhood trauma) share in the way of narrative structure? What do these stories reveal about the structure of social life?*
>
> (DeGloma 2014)

Meaning Consequences as Research Finding

While consequences of narrative productions of meaning can be an explicit question leading research, it also is common for research questions to be about topics other than narrative consequences yet for research *findings* to strongly suggest the presence and importance of consequences. Consider, for example, the following research question:

> *What are relationships between the kinds of stories asylum seekers are required to tell to be granted entry to the United States and the kinds of stories they typically have the abilities to tell?*
>
> (Bohmer and Schuman 2018)

The findings of this project supported the conclusion that the organizational characteristics of "good stories," those necessary to achieve asylum, are difficult—often impossible—for asylum seekers to tell. In consequence, asylum seekers often are simply unable to tell the kinds of stories that would gain them legal entry to the United States. The consequences are clear: Inability to tell the required story results in deportation from the United States.

Consider another example of how research not directly addressing consequences nonetheless can produce clear indications of effects of narrative productions of meaning:

How do paralegals guide Latina victims of domestic violence to tell the kinds of stories required for them to obtain legal protection?
(Trinch and Berk-Seligson 2002)

This research focused on the work of paralegal victim advocates who helped women shape their stories to meet organizational requirements. Findings empirically demonstrated how transforming women's personal stories into the organizational stories demanded by courts led women to obtain the court protection they desired. Again, the consequences of the meaning-making work of stories are clear and of practical importance: Organizational workers can assist clients in telling the right story, the story that will result in needed services.

In summary, there are important questions about story meaning regardless of who authors, tells, or evaluates stories, regardless of why or when or where stories are told: How is the content of a specific story or set of stories composed of particular systems of meaning (cultural and emotional codes)? What kinds of cognitive, emotional, and moral meanings do story contents produce? What are the characteristics of meanings evaluated as cognitively, emotionally, or morally persuasive—or as not persuasive—by particular audiences? In turn, answers to such questions are data to address a range of practical matters about what narrative meanings *do* for individuals, organizations, institutions, and culture; about whose interests these meanings serve; about how meanings are implicated in systems of social stratification, social order, and social change.

QUESTION TYPOLOGIES AND NARRATIVE RESEARCH IN PRACTICE

It should be clear from many of these examples that questions about narrative processes, contents, uses, relationships, and consequences often do *not* fit neatly into a typology of question types. Because this is centrally important for designing research I will offer two examples. Consider the following research question:

How do themes in children's books about Helen Keller and her teacher, Anne Sullivan, reflect and therefore perpetuate culturally circulating

stories about disability and, in so doing, ignore real-life complexity and
misrepresent the diverse characteristics of real people who are disabled?

(Souza 2020)

Notice how this question *assumes* the research examines story content (story "themes") in order to *compare* relationships among three types of narratives (those in culturally circulating stories about disability, those in children's books, the self-stories told by people with disabilities). The question points to interests in *consequences*: Culturally circulating stories about disability as well as themes in children's books misrepresent the diversity of actual experiences of those who are disabled. The conclusion of this research report developed the practical consequences of such misrepresentation.

A second example of how research questions guiding actual research do not fit neatly into specific categories is the following:

How do stories told by people experiencing disruption in their lives (such
as divorce, unemployment, death of a significant other) draw from
important cultural themes to help them reestablish order and continuity
in their lives?

(Becker 1997)

This question again assumes examination of content (the stories told by people experiencing disruption) and explicitly asks how this content reflects cultural systems of meaning ("important cultural themes"). The question also is about how narratives are used (to help reestablish order and continuity).

My point is simple yet essential: While I sorted questions into categories for presentation purposes, given the pervasiveness of stories on all levels of social life, it is not surprising that there are innumerable important research questions with countless variations. This multidimensionality and complexity offer considerable opportunities for researchers to be creative in developing the questions leading their research.

THE CENTRALITY OF QUESTIONS ABOUT STORY CONTENT

While not wishing to diminish the importance of questions about the activities and the actors involved in the social processes surrounding authoring, telling, and evaluating stories, here I focused on questions surrounding narrative meaning for two reasons. First, questions about narrative social processes can be adequately addressed using traditional social research techniques. Second, because our world increasingly is characterized by social, moral, and economic fragmentation, problems of meaning arise on all stages of social life. Therefore, the meaning-making capabilities of stories are of particular importance.

***

Chapters 1 and 2 have offered an outline for treating narrative as a topic of social research. I move now to guidelines for treating narrative as a method of social research.

NOTE

1.   See, for example, Boltanski (1999) and D'Andrade (1995).

NARRATIVE
AS RESEARCH
METHOD

3

NARRATIVE RESEARCH FOUNDATIONS

Illustrating the kinds of issues empirical research can explore about narrative productions of meaning leads to questions about the research process itself. The social scene for this discussion is complex because there are multiple, sometimes conflicting, images of social research in general, and narrative research in particular. I will begin by adopting a rather traditional definition of social research as a *systematic and empirical exploration of human social life*. *Systematic* means that the research process can be described in terms such as structured, orderly, methodical, consistent, and coherent. When research is systematic the steps taken throughout the research process can be fully described and adequately defended as logical. *Empirical* means research is evidence based. Unlike diaries, essays, or opinion pieces where authors simply assert arguments, research requires evidence from the social environment which can be sensed (in social research, primarily what can be seen or heard). *Human social life* is an all-encompassing term covering questions ranging from relationships between biological processes and social experiences to international governance.[1]

How can social researchers design, implement, and report empirical studies about narrative productions of meaning that will be evaluated as methodologically sound and therefore producing findings worthy of audience consideration? This chapter will develop the foundation for answers to this question: Sound research is that where every component of the research—from study questions, to samples, data generation methods, and analytic techniques—forms a *coherent* package. Critically, such coherence among elements of research design and implementation cannot be obtained simply by competent application of methodological techniques such as a good sample, survey, or interview or using the correct techniques of data analysis. Coherence rather is about being true to the philosophical foundations of research during all stages of research design and implementation.

In formal terms, this is about research *epistemology*, philosophical frameworks containing logical packages of ideas guiding images of the characteristics of the social world, the purposes of research, the kinds of questions research should address, preferred forms of data and analysis, and images of the characteristics of high-quality research. Although rarely explicitly covered in reports of research, and although often even a neglected topic in research methods textbooks, each of the practical elements of *any* research project—from research goals to study questions to samples to data analytic techniques—stands upon one or another philosophical foundation. My purpose in this chapter is to outline a philosophical framework capable of supporting empirical research on questions about the meanings made by stories in social life.[2] While seemingly abstract, this topic is of *practical* importance: Research incorporating elements of incompatible philosophical frameworks can be plagued by logical inconsistencies which make research findings incoherent and therefore not useful.

NATURALIST AND CONSTRUCTIONIST FOUNDATIONS OF RESEARCH

In broad outline, social research typically is led by one of two general philosophies, each beginning with specific images of the characteristics of the social world which logically lead to particular images of the purposes, topics, and goals of research. While these frameworks typically are referred to as "quantitative" and "qualitative," those terms invite misunderstandings because they direct attention only to differences in data form (numbers or words) and therefore obscure multiple differences that regularly are associated with data form.[3] I rather will use the expressions of "naturalist" and "constructionist" which better reflect the numerous differences in how frameworks conceptualize the social world and social research and how these, in turn, lead to predictable differences in research design, implementation, and evaluation. As will become clear, while naturalist philosophy does *not* easily support research on narrative meanings, its importance looms large so I begin there.

Naturalist Frameworks for Social Research

European and American social observers in the nineteenth and early twentieth centuries tended to develop social research in the model of natural sciences research. The *naturalist* philosophy underlying such research assumes the social world is the same as the natural world in that it (1) exists apart from human understandings and (2) is rule governed. Forming research in this mold leads to images that it is possible to (3) obtain measurements of the world that are precise and reproducible with the goal of (4) finding causal laws that explain broad patterns of events, characteristics, and behaviors. Finally, and again carrying over from the natural sciences, the image of researchers is of observers capable of recording and interpreting the world in ways that are (5) objective and impartial.

This naturalist framework historically was the first philosophy directing the design and implementation of social research and it remains both objectively and subjectively powerful. Naturalist philosophy is *objectively* powerful because it shapes *all* social research using experimental, survey, or statistical methodologies; it is the model of research all but required for publication in many top-rated social science journals, and is the form of research typically preferred by agencies funding large research projects. Additionally, local Institutional Review Boards typically require applicants for ethics approval to answer a series of questions pertinent to naturalist research, even when such questions are nonsensical for a particular research proposal. More subtly but as important, naturalist philosophy is *subjectively* powerful because its assumptions about the characteristics of the social world, of research, and of researchers often are the taken-for-granted assumptions about all social research throughout the social sciences. Glimmers of the subjective power of naturalist philosophy are reflected in how the value of "objectivity" typically is prized and "subjectivity" is scorned; in beliefs that a "truth" exists that can be measured. I shall return to the consequences of this subjective power when naturalist assumptions are used to evaluate research on narrative productions of meaning.

Naturalist Philosophy and Narrative Research

Many questions about narratives in social life reasonably *can* be framed within a naturalist framework. Such a frame, for example, can be justifiable to address questions about the characteristics of social actors who author, distribute, and evaluate stories, about how media shape story content, and about the characteristics of audiences likely to accept or reject the importance or believability of particular stories. Yet naturalist philosophy is *incompatible* with questions about narrative meaning: Naturalist research seeks to understand the objective world while story meaning is subjective; naturalist research seeks to reduce complexity while stories are valuable precisely because they can encompass the complexity of human experience. Further, "truth" within naturalist research is objective, singular, and measurable, while story "truth" is experiential, emotional, and moral. Still further, while the eyes and ears of naturalist researchers are assumed to be objective recorders and interpreters of the world, story content *always* is open to multiple interpretations influenced by the personal characteristics and life experiences of story evaluators—including those of researchers.

Given this, it is *not possible* to design sensible research on questions of narrative meaning within a naturalist framework.[4]

Constructionist Frameworks for Social Research

Although naturalist philosophy has an impressive record of accomplishments in guiding research exploring questions about the physical world, the philosophy is associated with multiple problems when used to direct research on questions about the social world.[5] *Constructionism* is a research philosophy historically developed in *explicit* opposition to naturalism.

Constructionist research begins with an image that (1) meaning does not reside in persons, objects, events, or experiences but rather is a human creation. Given this, (2) the goal of research is to understand how humans create that meaning. Most certainly, constructionist philosophy does *not* deny the existence of physical realities. That would be absurd. Rather, what this philosophy does is (3) direct attention away from material characteristics of people, objects, experiences, and events toward the *subjective processes of meaning-making*. Further, while naturalist philosophy assumes the independent existence of material realities, constructionist philosophy rather (4) supports examining the subjective and material characteristics of the social world as the *consequences* of meaning-making. Finally, rather than images of researchers as human audiovisual recorders, researchers within constructionism are assumed to be (5) practical actors whose own characteristics, experiences, and values will shape their perceptions and understandings of the social world and therefore influence how they design and implement research, as well as how they make sense of study findings.[6]

In summary, constructionist philosophy supports research on a variety of questions about *how* stories create meanings, about *what* meanings stories create, as well as how story meanings do the *work* of sensemaking on all stages of social life.

RESEARCH FOUNDATIONS AND RESEARCH PRACTICES

Although rudimentary, my description of the two most typical philosophical frameworks supporting social research allows considering how specific philosophies lead to a variety of differences in research design, implementation, data analysis, and presentation of research results. I will start with a straightforward example: The goal of the naturalist research is to find general patterns. Logically, only relatively large samples are capable of finding such patterns, which means preferred data are in the form of *numbers* because only numbers are capable of describing large quantities. Yet, the logic—and ensuing problematics—of mathematical measurement rightfully leads to concern about the extent to which mathematical differences found in data are real (measuring something that truly exists) or are mere artifacts of statistical procedures. This logically leads to relying on measures of *statistical significance* (differences that likely are more real than random) which, in turn, requires samples that are both large and random. Hence, large, random samples and statistical analysis of quantitative data are the ideal model for research based on a foundation of naturalist philosophy. The point: *This is a logical package.*

Contrast that particular package of assumptions and expectations with constructionist frameworks focused on exploring questions about meaning. Preferred data for such topics must be in the form of words because only words are capable of grasping the subtle, complex nature of meaning. Further, because constructionist philosophy maintains that patterns exist only through human meaning-making, and because meaning and the processes of meaning-making *always* are contextualized, large samples are neither expected nor praised because statistical generalizability is *not* possible, and therefore *not* a research goal. Again, this is a *logical package* beginning with philosophical assumptions about the world and ending in practical guidelines for research design.

Naturalist and constructionist philosophies also lead to different expectations about *researchers*. Within naturalism, researchers are to be "objective" recorders and interpreters of facts which exist independently in the world. In research practice, such objectivity sometimes is simply assumed and sometimes is enforced by design components such as double-blind experiments or intercoder reliability checks. In contrast, constructionist philosophy assumes there can be no "objectivity" in apprehending the social world because perceptions and understandings necessarily are contextualized: What we see and hear depend upon who we are, where we are, why we are observing, and so on. This leads constructionist research to avoid claims of objectivity and to take seriously the ways in which researcher social positions, personal characteristics, and life experiences might influence their observations and interpretations. In turn, this leads to emphasizing how researchers must seriously consider and honestly report the ways in which their research decisions (what to research, how to measure, how to analyze data, and so on) likely are influenced by their personal experiences, characteristics, and values.[7]

Communication conventions is a third difference associated with philosophical frameworks underlying research. Naturalist inspired research tends to follow the communications customs of research in the natural sciences. This communication form privileges linear arguments supported by statistics presented in short sentences. Such writing also tends to be in the third person passive voice which is understandable given the framework's image of researchers as simply recorders of the facts existing in the material world. In comparison, constructionist research tends to be written in ways more literary than scientific. As compared to scientific writing, reports of constructionist research often contain sentences that are longer and more descriptive; arguments are supported by the strength of logic as well as by the quality and quantity of data examples presented to exemplify the line of reasoning. Not surprisingly, writing often is in a first person, active voice reflecting assumptions that researchers are active participants in the research process.[8]

In summary, naturalist and constructionist philosophies pose different images of the social world, different questions about that world, and different ideas about the purposes and implementation of research. To be absolutely clear, it does *not* make sense to argue that one or another philosophy is "better." Each leads to research designs suited for examining some kinds of questions—and not others; each carries a range of positive—and negative—theoretical and practical consequences when used to direct social research.

Research Foundations and Research Evaluation

Differences in philosophies underlying research also inform the evaluation of research *quality*. Criteria to evaluate naturalist research are fairly standard and agreed upon. Most social research textbooks contain a fairly standard list of these criteria such as the ability of samples to support statistical generalization, indicators of multiple forms of reliability and validity, and so on. Not so with constructionist research where there are multiple visions of what, precisely, constitutes research quality in the first place as well as of how such quality can be assessed.

Rather than enter debates about specific criteria for evaluating the quality of constructionist research, I will offer three observations that each have practical implications for designing and conducting research. First, constructionist researchers sometimes argue that there are no agreed-upon criteria for judging research quality because there *can* be no criteria as criteria of any type would stifle the creativity that constructionists believe is a prized hallmark of their research. While there is truth to the allegation that evaluative criteria of any kind encourage uniformity rather than creativity, such an argument denies the reality that constructionist research is *routinely* evaluated: Student work is evaluated by faculty; the work of professionals is evaluated by editors and reviewers, conference organizers, members of awards committees, and so on. My first observation is that denying the possibility of evaluating constructionist research quality denies the reality that research quality is routinely evaluated. Denying evaluative criteria also encourages unsystematic analysis which dooms research to remain on the borders of methodological acceptability.[9]

My second observation is that there are common problems with criteria used to evaluate constructionist research. Given that there is little agreement about what, specifically, constitutes high-quality constructionist research, evaluators can use *different criteria* to assess the same manuscript which can lead to wildly divergent evaluations. Additionally, given the subjective powers of naturalist philosophy, evaluators sometimes use the *wrong criteria* to appraise a constructionist manuscript. When constructionist research is evaluated through naturalist criteria the predictable evaluation is that the research is hopelessly flawed.

This leads to my third observation. It is all too common for research on narrative to be fundamentally unsound because researchers asking constructionist-inspired questions about meaning nonetheless frame components of their research within naturalist philosophy.[10] Such manuscripts are recognizable: They can include heroic efforts to justify very small samples as nonetheless generalizable, or contain tables of numerical counts even if most cells show a count of 0 or 1, or present statistics that are senseless given small numbers. Most commonly, manuscripts asking constructionist questions within naturalist frameworks end with lengthy "limitations" sections primarily apologizing for the ways in which the research does not conform to naturalist standards. Part naturalist and part constructionist, such research is fully neither. In consequence, and almost by definition, these manuscripts are evaluated through either naturalist or constructionist criteria as not high quality.

Research Foundations and Research Design

How can researchers most productively deal with the practical problems surrounding research (on any topic) informed by constructionist philosophy within a world objectively and subjectively privileging research designed within naturalist frameworks?

First, researchers should be aware that differences between naturalist and constructionist philosophy and models of research are about far more than whether data are in the form of numbers or words. Remember there are multiple differences between two contending frameworks underlying all elements of research design and implementation.

Second, it sometimes is possible to do creative "mixing and matching" of constructionist and naturalist elements in one research project. While this can create innovative ways to approach research questions, such mixing and matching more often leads to research design that is not coherent and therefore to findings that are too easily dismissible. The lesson for researchers is obvious: Mix elements of philosophical frameworks knowingly and with care.

Third, given the objective and subjective power of naturalist frameworks and, given a lack of agreement about constructionist evaluative criteria, constructionist researchers should be *particularly diligent* about both doing and communicating issues of research design, implementation, and analysis. This requires anticipating reader questions as well as carefully justifying design and analytic decisions.

Finally, constructionist researchers should *not* take scarce manuscript pages to apologize for the ways in which characteristics of their research departs from those associated with naturalistic frameworks. Such apologies can be interpreted as researchers' negative evaluations of their own research and therefore invite questions about why the research was done if it is so flawed. It is far more productive to use the space to explain to readers the ways in which study questions and study methods are *logical* and the ways in which the research process was *systematic*.

In summary, any social research project organized within constructionist frameworks exists in a world where the competing naturalist framework is both practically and subjectively powerful. Researchers familiar with frameworks and their consequences can take steps to encourage readers to evaluate their studies as sound and their findings worthy of consideration.

There is a further foundational issue underlying empirical examinations of narrative productions of meaning: Such questions require researchers to be sensitive to the particular issues posed by meaning as an empirical question.

MEANING AS EMPIRICAL QUESTION

How can questions about narrative meaning be empirically explored in ways that are methodologically sound? Within naturalist frameworks, this question has a straightforward and agreed-upon answer: It is the task of researchers to find the meanings that reside in persons, objects, events, and experiences. Within naturalist frameworks, a central mark of sound research is "validity," achieved when researchers convince their audiences that the meanings they have located in their data correspond to the meanings that actually exist in the material world.

Issues surrounding empirical explorations of meaning are vastly more complicated when meaning is understood as something people create, rather than as something that exists in persons, objects, events, and experiences. As such, it makes *no* sense to ask about the extent to which study findings reflect "real" characteristics in the world. Further, when meaning is understood as contextualized then it resides only in the eyes of the beholder. What a person, object, event, or experience "means" depends upon whom is making the assessment, on why and where and when the assessment is being made, upon how the target of the assessment (person, object, event, experience) is understood as embedded in time and place, and so on.

Such a philosophical frame leads to substantial problems in designing and implementing research. How can research be other than highly specific, tightly confined, narrowly focused case studies? How can there be any accumulation of knowledge about meanings or the processes of meaning creation? If meaning is in the eyes of the beholder, how is it possible to achieve any measure of agreement on the extent to which a manuscript reporting research contains a defensible interpretation of data?

Some researchers circumvent such problems by simply ignoring them and proceeding as if problems do not exist. This, however, has troublesome consequences: Findings can be evaluated as too simplistic because they fail to acknowledge the complexity of meanings and meaning creation processes; likely influences of researchers' world views and circumstances are ignored which invites audience questions about unacknowledged biases and their consequences.

At the other end of the spectrum of responses to dilemmas created by the complexity of meaning are researchers who design very narrowly focused case studies featuring interpretations of data explicitly defined as reflecting merely the opinion of the researcher as well as warnings that study findings cannot be taken to reflect anything about the general characteristics of meaning or meaning-making processes. This, too, has unfortunate consequences: It produces research so narrow in scope that it is of interest to very small audiences; it tends to focus more on the characteristics of the researcher than on the data; it leads to endless case studies that do not build upon one another.

Meaning and Research Design

It *is* possible to design sound research that avoids the extremes of either jettisoning constructionist understandings of meaning or embracing them to the point that researchers become paralyzed with fear about generalization or their own biases. My suggestions are similar to those about increasing the likelihood that constructionist research will be evaluated as worthwhile and sound within a world where the values and assumptions of naturalist frameworks are objectively and subjectively powerful.

First and foremost, sound research (of any type) requires being particularly attentive to the practical steps taken to do the research as well as in clearly communicating these steps to the anticipated audience. Second, it requires acknowledging the problems of investigating meaning yet taking these to justify caution rather than immobilization. Third, it requires acknowledging the ways in which researchers' personal characteristics and circumstances likely influence understandings, and being mindful of these in the process of doing the research, while not making the research more about the researcher than about the research topic. These three suggestions rest upon a fourth which is, by far, the most important: Analysts must proceed with a healthy dose of modesty within a mindset that they are seeking to explore the mysteries of social life, not experts who already know the secrets locked in the data.

FOUNDATIONS OF RESEARCH PRACTICE

While social research textbooks typically focus on practical techniques of data analysis (such as *how* to choose samples, write interview questions, or organize codebooks), my hope is that this chapter encourages researchers to understand the importance of a range of concerns underlying the concrete practices of research design and implementation. True, such topics rarely are contained in final manuscripts reporting research. Yet considering research fundamentals is time well spent because research evaluated as sound will rest on a firm foundation and such foundations cannot be created merely through technical competence in using analytic techniques.

I turn now to a variety of practical dimensions for accomplishing the goal of designing and implementing sound empirical research on narrative productions of meaning.

NOTES

1. My definition of social research is generic in that it does *not* distinguish research according to where it is done or to why it is done, according to any specific theoretical or political stance, or to any particular understanding of the requirements of "evidence." In practice, different audiences have widely differing expectations of what constitutes sound research so researchers do well to pay attention to the requirements associated with their intended audiences.

2. I will offer merely an outline of what is central to the practical tasks of designing, conducting, and evaluating research and refer readers elsewhere for more complete discussions. For example, *Ways of Knowing: Competing Methodologies in Social and Political Research* by Jonathon Moses and Torbjørn Knutsen (2012) is a book-length discussion of the histories of constructionist and naturalist research philosophies; Crotty (2015), Gusfield (1990), and Loseke (2017) offer summaries of what lies behind the practical techniques of social research design and implementation.

3. In use, "quantitative" most often is associated with research that is deductive in logic, as well as survey or experimental in form while "qualitative" is associated with research that is inductive in logic and interview or observational in form. However, such associations are not invariable: An experiment, for example, can use verbal data to measure the dependent variable; interviews can be coded and words can be translated into numerical representations, and so on.

4. Research questions about narrative content *can* be examined within naturalist frameworks by assuming that meaning is fixed and resides in persons, objects, or events. Such a stance supports asking about the frequency of particular words or phrases, or the extent to which particular words or phrases appear together. David Altheide's work (2002) on how newspaper formats can encourage public fear is a good example of such research; Perrier and Gines (2018) review narrative research in the health sciences, much of which uses experimental methodologies.

5. Summaries of problems associated with research guided by naturalist perspectives within social science can be found in Calhoun and VanAntwerpen (2007), Loseke (2019), and Steinmetz (2005).

6. Fairly accessible summaries of social constructionist frameworks include: Burr (2015), Gergen (1994), Lock and Strong (2010), and Weinberg (2014).

7. Qualitative researchers working within critical perspectives pay considerable attention to researchers' "positionality," primarily to the consequences of researchers' race/class/gender/sexuality on the research process. The constructionist framework includes this as well as sensitivity to how a range of other considerations (such as ability/disability, age, personal experiences, and so on) influence perception and understandings.

8. Joseph Gusfield (1990) offers an examination of these differences through comparing the style and arguments of two books that both have the status of "classics" within sociology: The *American Occupational Structure* (Blau and Duncan) which is in the naturalist tradition, and *Talley's Corner* (Liebow) in the constructionist tradition.

9. See, for example, Seale (2004), and Atkinson and Delamont (2006).

10. Sometimes this unfortunate muddle of naturalist and constructionist visions arises because researchers have interests in examining narrative productions of meanings, yet are familiar only with the naturalist framework; sometimes it is because researchers anticipate that naturalist criteria will be used by reviewers so they attempt to mold research in ways seeming to meet those expectations.

4 NARRATIVE RESEARCH PRACTICES

The previous chapter focused on the underlying foundations of research practices. While rarely a topic in reports of research, philosophical and theoretical frameworks are the scaffolding underlying sound research design and implementation. This chapter turns to more practical aspects of research about narrative productions of meaning. I will start with how the characteristics of stories somewhat automatically lead to particular orientations toward data and data analysis and continue with analytic strategies (close reading and data categorization) and analytic tasks (contextualizing story production and research questions). I will conclude with some comments about communication tactics.[1]

ORIENTATIONS TO NARRATIVE DATA AND ANALYSIS

Three characteristics of stories shape typical orientations to data analysis. First, stories are a powerful form of communication because they can appeal to the *complexities* of social life. This means that stories are not always—perhaps not even usually—clear in their images of people, objects, events, and experiences.[2] In consequence, researchers should *not* enter the process of data analysis with assumptions that story characters will be instances of stock narrative characters such as victims, villains, or heroes or that story events will yield a clear, unified, unambiguous plot. On the contrary. Many of the most widely circulating stories are interesting precisely because characters are complex and unpredictable, because story plots and morals are ambiguous, because the stories can be understood as containing apparently contradictory meanings. So, in stark comparison to the kinds of findings preferred within naturalist research, the goal of narrative research is *not* producing an analysis that erases the complexity and ambiguity of life.

Second, stories can achieve their power through appealing to cognition, to emotion, and/or to moral sensibilities.[3] In consequence, researchers should not simply dismiss stories seeming to offer their audiences a distinctly nonfactual view of the world. The power of such stories might rather be obtained through appeals to emotion and/or moral evaluation.

Third, recall that the characteristics and meanings of story settings, characters, plots, and morals depend upon the characteristics, understandings, and experiences of audiences (including the researcher) doing the interpretations and evaluations. In consequence, *any* question about *any* set of stories can have a range of *equally justifiable* answers. As such, the process of analysis is not about finding the "right" answer to a research question. Rather, the goal of analysis is forming answers that are *true* to the data, as well as *logical* and *coherent*.

STORIES AS RESEARCH DATA

Two major issues surround the topic of stories as research data. First, the taken-for-granted nature of the story form on all stages of social life makes it necessary to define "story" for the purposes of social research. Second, for a variety of reasons, research about narrative productions of meaning rarely attempts statistical generalization of study findings. Nonetheless, it is important to carefully think through the processes and likely consequences of story selection and the number of stories examined.

Conceptualizing "Stories" for Research

How can particular objects in the social world be recognized as "stories?" The short answer is that, despite remarkable variation, stories contain some combination of scenes, characters, and events that are both contextualized and coordinated in ways creating cognitive, emotional, and/or moral meanings. Stories typically of interest to social researchers also are those told as *true* (regardless of any relationship between the story and truth as objectively measured) and they contain *human* characters. Useful for social research are stories created as stories as well as stories created by researchers.

Stories Created as Stories

Many stories told on all stages of private and public life require no instruction for how they can be recognized as stories because they are relatively free-standing communication forms explicitly told as stories. In such cases researchers can rely on their practical experiences and common sense to identify these as "stories" that can serve as data for social research.

Researcher Created Stories

The concept of "story" for social research can be enlarged to include more than the obvious "story told as a story." Researchers themselves can create the stories they then analyze by combining stories told as stories or by creating stories from other materials not explicitly offered as stories.

First, researchers can combine several instances of *particular* stories to produce a more *general* story form. In this way, a collection of stories on the GoFundMe website can be used to examine the characteristics of self-stories told by those requesting help from others; stories of specific individuals experiencing psychological trouble can be combined to explore a variety of questions about the meanings of mental illness; stories of particular people enticed into a life of crime can be used to tell the story of entering a life of crime, and so on. In these instances, unique stories, or fragments of unique stories, are combined by researchers to compose what is then taken as a more general story.

Second, chunks of communication can be examined as a story even though audiences are not explicitly instructed to evaluate the communication in this way. It can make sense, for instance, to conceptualize a website, a speech, a meeting, a public hearing, or a blog as a story and ask questions about the images of characters, plots, and morals it conveys. This is the traditional work of ethnographers who use data from a variety of sources (such as interviews, observations, document analysis) to piece together a story of an organization or event; it is the work of historians who examine a range of documents for how they create images (stories) of particular historical eras. Chapter 6 demonstrates how Congressional testimony not in storied form nonetheless can be examined as containing the story of the American Dream.

Researchers therefore can construct more general stories from particular stories; they can conceptualize blocks of communication as stories even though they are not presented as such. Researchers creating such data, of course, must justify to their audiences the ways in which it makes sense to treat particular segments of communication as a story although they were not authored as such; they must justify the ways in which it makes sense to assume that a group of stories shares sufficient form or content to be conceptualized as one type of story.

Locating Stories for Examination

Where can stories be found? I will briefly attend to the question of sites of story production because narrative researchers tend to gravitate toward personally conducted, in-depth, unstructured interviews. While such data have the distinct advantage of directly addressing the specific research questions of interest, they can create significant restrictions on research. For example, the time and effort needed to locate respondents, as well as to arrange, do, and transcribe interviews makes interviewing a very labor- and time-intensive form of data generation. So, unless blessed with substantial funding and time, interviewing limits the number of people who can be interviewed and hence the amount of data that can be generated. Projects relying on very small amounts of data can yield analysis that seem thin, inviting questions about the extent to which anything meaningful can be empirically supported. Further, interview data are best suited to addressing social psychological questions about individual meaning, and less suited to exploring myriad questions about organizational or institutional meanings or about the social and political work of stories in public life. Such limitations justify expanding images of data for narrative analysis beyond that obtained from researcher-conducted interviews.

Stories are pervasive on all stages of social life, so they can be found throughout the social world. Stories told as stories and other communication that reasonably can be shaped into story form are found in: social advocacy documents, published autobiographies, diaries (including blogs), organizational documents and brochures, testimony in courts and public policy hearings, lectures, sermons and speeches, advertisements, and media of all varieties. The web contains an increasing number of sites dedicated to collecting stories of people with particular characteristics or problems such as those who are adult and child survivors of abuse, immigrants, veterans, disabled, anorexic teens, absentee fathers, trans, punks, poor people, people who overcame poverty as well as those currently living in poverty, chronically ill, end-of-life, first-generation college students, teachers, and so on.

We live in a world saturated with stories which means a virtual goldmine of stories exists on all stages of social life. These offer researchers countless opportunities to expand data beyond that generated through the very time consuming process of researcher-conducted interviews.

Selecting Stories for Examination

While studies not seeking statistical generalization are freed from the need to establish samples that are large enough and representative enough to support statistical generation, it is absolutely essential to inform audience members how and why particular stories—and not others—were chosen for analysis. Readers must be convinced that the stories selected for examination are capable of addressing the research questions. While what, specifically, this means depends upon the characteristics of the particular research project, some general points inform decisions about data selection.

First, regardless of whether data come from interviews generated by the researcher or from publicly available stories generated by others for purposes other than research, characteristics of the data *source* always at least somewhat influence—and sometimes completely determine—likely story contents. Further, when some stories *are* selected for examination, others are *not* selected and this raises questions about the ways in which story selection might/likely/definitely influence study findings. Given the practical consequences of both story source and story selection procedures, it is *not* warranted to simply ignore questions about where and how stories were selected simply because statistical generalization is not a research goal. Sound research requires researchers to think through the ways in which characteristics of where and how data were selected might/likely/definitely inform the kinds of stories that are told—and that are not told, and the ways in which this likely does—or does not—shape study findings. Chapters 5 and 6 include demonstrations of these considerations.

Second, researchers must convince audiences that the stories used as data are, in some way, *significant*. After all, while an all but infinite number of stories are told on all stages of social life, only some have any significance for anyone. Sound research will be based on data that are, in one way or another, not trivial. For example, countless blogs appear and just as quickly disappear and are read by few, if any, people other than their authors. How is it possible to argue stories from such a blog reflect anything other than a blogger's world view? A blog becomes important if, for example, it is written by a person important for one or another reason, is read by a considerable number of people, or by people in a particular audience of interest, is frequently cited (by politicians, educators, commentators, by those in some group of interest, and so on), is an "official" blog of someone or something of interest, is the longest running blog, the first blog of a particular sort, and so on. There are countless ways in which a story or group of stories might be significant, and there is not an agreed-upon set of criteria to judge social significance. Therefore, what stories are—and are not—worthy of empirical research is a subjective judgment rather than an objective description. It is up to researchers to convince their audiences that the data represent something that is worthy of examination.

Third, researchers should follow practices associated with social research of all varieties and convey to audiences how items in a collection of stories were selected. When data are researcher generated from interviews or surveys, audiences should be told how respondents were selected and how interviews were conducted. Storied data not generated by researchers likewise require informing audiences about what led the researcher to take interest in a particular site, be it a web page, media event, organization, or set of documents; what rules shaped the selection of stories into the sample; how rules for inclusion simultaneously led some stories to not being selected and resulting likely biases from all these decisions as well as the ways in which these biases likely do—or do not—matter in the analysis. Again, while there is *no* need to apologize for the ways in which a selection of stories is not "random," it *is* important to convince readers that the collection of stories was not haphazard; that there were rules for selecting the data; and that these rules are justifiable. Chapters 5 and 6 demonstrate these types of considerations.

Determining Data Quantity

Because statistical generalization is not a research goal, narrative research does *not* need to examine an amount of data mathematically necessary to support statistical procedures. Hence, there is no formal need for large samples, or for apologizing that samples are not as large as those associated with research using statistical analysis. Yet this cannot be taken as a justification for ignoring questions about the number of stories needed: Data must be of *sufficient magnitude* to warrant making whatever conclusions are made.

Disagreements about the number of cases needed for a sound narrative analysis is a common reason why reviewers come to different conclusions about the adequacy of any particular data set. As such, it is the reason why researchers must take seriously the task of convincing their audiences that the analysis is built on an empirical foundation strong enough to support assertions being made. Most critically, this is *not* an argument that can be made on the strength of numbers alone. That is, although within naturalist frameworks the general rule is the more cases the better, the verbal data associated with constructionist frameworks severely limit the amount of data (in this case, number of stories) that can be analyzed. Simply put, the greater the number of stories examined, the less comprehensive the analysis can be. Trading increasing number of stories for decreasing comprehensiveness of data analysis can be an ill-advised exchange. Once again, it is the task of the researcher to convince audiences that the collection of stories being examined is large enough to support conclusions.

I turn now to analytic strategies and tasks surrounding empirical examinations of narrative productions of meaning.

ANALYTIC STRATEGIES

Regardless of particular research questions, and regardless of the particular characteristics of storied data, narrative analysis of meaning *always* and *necessarily* rests upon two analytic strategies that are fundamental to all empirical work using words as data: close reading and data categorization.[4] Chapters 5–7 each offers detailed examples of these strategies.

Close Reading

All techniques for empirically examining narrative productions of meaning rest upon *close reading* which is far different from the often haphazard ways we approach reading in daily life where we tend to read novels, webpages, and so on as quickly as we can; where we skim over what seems uninteresting and rarely pause to ask how arguments are being made, the extent to which the sentences and paragraphs hang together to form a cohesive whole, what sorts of values they reflect, whose interests they serve, and so forth. In stark contrast, analysis of verbal data necessarily depends upon close reading which is, first and foremost, slow and careful reading in order to notice the smallest of details which can be critical in shaping the meaning of stories as well as in understanding how stories achieve their cognitive, emotional, and/or moral persuasiveness.

Needless to say, close reading is very time consuming because it is about paying attention to the smallest of details. What this means in practice is that researchers slowly and carefully read their data multiple times. The first readings are to gain familiarity with story generalities; subsequent readings identify themes which are recurring images in story scenes, characters, and/or events; later readings refine initial impressions. Close reading is sensitive to how the story is put together, to how the use of one word rather than another encourages or discourages particular kinds of cognitive or emotional responses, to the amount of time/space given to describing one event rather than another; to how a particular event is placed within a series of events, what sorts of visions of the world the story reflects, perpetuates, challenges, and so on. Close reading also is sensitive to story *silences*: What characters or events might be expected in a story of this type yet are absent and with what consequences? How, and in what ways do particular patterns of silences have likely meaningful consequences to a story's cognitive, emotional, moral meaning?

Within constructionist frameworks it is a truism that meaning is what people create, not something that resides within objects, events, or people. As such, researchers are *creating* story meaning rather than *finding* it. What kinds of meaning are attributed to stories depend, in part, on the *stance* directing the reading.[5] Constructionist frameworks renounce the possibility of an "objective" (unbiased) stance promoted within naturalism and rather promote other kinds of orientations toward reading. A *literal* stance requires remaining tightly focused on the surface of the story, taking story statements quite literally and not looking behind them for meanings lurking in the background or reading people or events into the story that are not explicitly contained in the story. In comparison, an *imposture* reading centers on how story plots, characters, and morals are embedded in cultural and political structures. Finally, an *oppositional* reading reflects researchers' orienting bias that literal meanings are fraudulent (they do not represent a reality as objectively measured) and knowingly organized in ways that deceive, so the reading is focused on locating moments of deception.[6] Regardless of the stance, close reading requires approaching data in ways that are *explicit*. Researchers should think through the stance they are using to read the stories, as well as the likely biases and consequences of that stance and inform their audiences of both stance and consequence.

Data Categorization

The second data analytic foundation is *categorization*.[7] Categorization in daily life is quite routine and done without reflection: Grapes, pineapples, and pears can be categorized as fruit; fruit, meat, and chocolate can be categorized as food; food and water and air can be categorized as necessary for human survival; and so on.

The analytic process of categorization takes *specific* story elements (elements of scenes, characters, events) and categorizes them into *types* of scenes, characters, and events. At times, this process is as straightforward as the categorization of mundane objects in daily life: Story characters of "mom" and "sister" and "brother" can be categorized as "family"; story scenes containing behaviors of "pushes" and "shoves" and "beatings" can be categorized as "violence." Yet many of the most important classifications are not so routine because they rest upon *moral* evaluations: Are multidimensional and unique people without legal citizenship or documentation categorized as "good, hardworking Americans" or "criminal aliens?" What particular story events are those of "microaggressions?" Story scenes, characters, and events do not come with labels describing their cognitive, emotional, or moral meanings. These meanings are the consequence of categorization, an analytic task. Perceived story meanings are the consequence of researchers' categorization.

When data are verbal, it is words that require categorization; when data are visual it is images. Regardless, the task is to look at the content of stories—words, sentences, paragraphs, or images—and decide which of them might be logically combined as a subtype of a larger idea and which others can be combined as a subtype of another larger idea, and so on.[8] As in all things related to research, the process of data categorization must be logical and systematic.

That said, while maintaining the goal of analytic practice as logical and systematic, it is most certain that the actual process of categorization often seems more art than science. No set of fixed rules or procedures can adequately lead analysis because *everything* about stories is contextualized. In consequence, perceived cognitive, emotional, and moral meanings of elements in a specific story or in a set of stories "depends." Given this, while researchers can find software programs for qualitative data analysis to be helpful in "finding" instances of specific words or sets of words, such programs can find only what they are instructed to find. It is researchers who must do the work of categorization, work that relies on the practices of close reading.

In summary, the analytic strategy of categorization is that of asserting commonalities which, depending upon the data and the research questions, might be commonalities among elements (scenes, characters, events, plots, morals) within one story or commonalities among elements of several stories. Although categorization is about commonalities, researchers also should be attuned to *variations*. Unlike statistics where variations are treated as outliers and ignored or are mathematically brought into line, one reason why stories are an important and powerful communication form is that, as compared to logical arguments, charts, graphs, or statistical tables, stories have greater potentials to portray the messiness of social life. Categorization should *not* seek to erase messiness: Relatively few story characters, for example, are "pure" victims or villains or heroes. Do not create story characters as archetypical narrative characters or transform story events into archetypical narrative events. Formula stories and analyst-created typologies should not become boxes into which data are stuffed.

Finally, yet critically, insights from multiple close readings as well as from various attempts at different forms of data categorizations should be thoroughly *documented* in written form. It is this documentation that will become the basis for communicating both the process and the outcomes of data analysis.

Close reading and data categorization are fundamental techniques to examine *any* set of data in the form of words, whether or not those words are in the form of stories. Unlike statistical procedures, these strategies are *not* a predetermined series of steps taken in a particular order. Yet while more art than science in form, these strategies are similar to statistical procedures in that both should be *systematic*.

ANALYTIC TASKS

Some aspects of narrative analysis are those of qualitative analyses in general: Researchers do rigorous close readings; they categorize data in order to answer research questions. Because a distinctive feature of narrative is that story meaning is *contextualized*, narrative analysis also must attend to the social contexts of story production as well as to how the story elements that are a focus of research are contextualized within the stories being examined. Each of the chapters in Part III demonstrates aspects of the practical work of contextualization.

Contextualizing Story Production

Regardless of the specific research question or data characteristics, analysts must establish the *social contexts* of story creation. When research questions themselves are about such a context, systematically exploring the following will be the primary method/goal of data analysis. When research questions are not about the social contexts of story production, it nonetheless is important to take these contexts seriously because narrative meaning *always* is contextual.

Understanding story meanings requires placing perceived story content within various contexts of their production, and it is beneficial from the earliest stages of data analysis to think through how each of these influences the ways the stories being examined are constructed as well as how the kinds of appeals (cognitive, emotional, moral) such stories might have for these stories likely are evaluated by audiences with different characteristics. While not all of the following are pertinent and/or possible to explore in specific stories or sets of stories, and while only those contexts that are important to the analysis need be reported in final manuscripts, the more the following can be explored and become a part of researchers' understandings of their data, the better. As with close reading and data categorization, findings and insights should be documented in written form so they can be consulted throughout the process of data analysis.

What are the probable biases in the collection of stories being examined and what are their likely consequences? There is no such thing as an "unbiased" collection of stories. Without exception, stories reflect biases from *who* tells the story, from *where* and *when*, and to *whom* stories are told. What requires attention, therefore, are possible/probable biases as well as how these biases possibly/probably/necessarily effect story characteristics. Critically, not all biases are of equal importance. Some might not be important at all to a particular research project, others might be exceptionally important.

Who authored the story? Story authorship is important because authors with different social statuses, personal characteristics, and agendas tell starkly different stories. Yet story authorship can be difficult to know, especially when researchers use stories written by others. A primary example of the often slippery nature of story authorship is stories *told* as self-narratives yet authored by others such as organizational workers telling stories about their clients, teachers or parents telling stories about children, or support group leaders telling stories about group members. Additionally, stories circulating through media often are repeatedly modified through multiple retellings so it is not possible to attribute a particular story to a particular person or organization. Analysts do well to think through implications of authorship for story characteristics as well as about how stories might have been modified through repeated retellings.

To what extent are stories personal/organizational/institutional or cultural narratives? An initial task in working with narrative data is determining the extent to which stories are instances of personal, organizational, institutional, or cultural narratives because stories authored on different stages of social life have different characteristics and, for the most part, do different kinds of work. It is important to remember that, although it is possible to *analytically* distinguish among narratives produced on different stages of social life, in practice, each type of narrative influences and is influenced by each other and any story commonly has elements of two or more narrative types. Examine stories for their inclusions of different forms of narratives and consider likely implications of personal stories embedded in organizational stories, cultural stories embedded in institutional stories, and so on.

Why was the story authored? Stories are authored for different reasons and, if possible, it is good to know why the story was authored. At times, this is fairly straightforward because authors often *explicitly* inform their audiences why the story was authored; at other times the purpose of a story is clear from *where* it is located. It is, for example, logical to assume stories appearing in advertisements are there to sell a product be it pears or politicians; it is logical to assume stories appearing in textbooks are to educate, that stories told by clergy are to demonstrate a moral lesson, and so on. I offer two cautions. First, blurred genres (infotainment, infomercial) increasingly characterize public life which can make it difficult to easily categorize story purpose. Second, it is not particularly beneficial to speculate about psychological motives driving story production: Psychological motives are unknowable and also not helpful in understanding the social nature of story production and consumption.

Who is the intended audience? The probable/possible meanings of stories and the probability that a story is evaluated as believable and important depend on characteristics of audiences doing the evaluation. Story audiences can be multiple in the current era where media of all varieties make it possible for stories to circulate far beyond their intended audiences. Hence, consider the characteristics and consequences of stories that have two (or more) audiences: Those for whom the story was written and those encountering the story through media of any variety.

What is the personal relationship of the researcher to this audience and this story? Thus far, I have been implicitly critical of researchers who are so concerned with how their own circumstances and characteristics influence their work that the research becomes more about the researcher than about the topic. Yet *far more troubling* is failure to reflect enough about how researchers' own circumstances and understandings influence every dimension of research from forming study questions to data selection to data analysis. As I have said repeatedly and will say once more: While it is *not* possible to eliminate consequences of researcher biases, it *is* possible to be particularly attentive to this issue at every step of the research process and to be honest in recognizing biases, in admitting the probable strength and direction of their influences on the research, and in reporting this to audiences.

Contextualizing Research Questions

Data analysis should begin by contextualizing particular research questions within the *general* characteristics of the storied data. This will be the central issue for data analysis when research questions explicitly are about story characteristics. Yet even then, because research questions most often focus on one or another specific, often very narrowly defined, story component, it remains useful to establish the *general* characteristics of stories being examined before moving on to exploring what is necessary to address particular research questions.

There are innumerable possible questions that might be important to ask about story characteristics; relevant specific questions depend upon characteristics of the particular collection of stories being examined as well as characteristics of the particular research questions. Among often essential characteristics are the following: To what extent are the storied data *offered* as "true," regardless of any relationship to truth as objectively or scientifically measured? What are the most important characteristics (physical, social, political, geographical) of the story scene? What cultural codes (symbolic, emotion) are central in shaping the story? To what extent are these codes important to general audiences and/or to specific audiences? Who are the main story characters? To what extent are these characters unique, embodied people or types of people? To what extent are these characters instances of archetypical narrative characters (such as victim, villain, hero, fool)? What sorts of moral evaluations of these characters are encouraged? What is/are the most important plots and subplots? What are the morals of the story?

Crucially, story contents can be shaped by what is *excluded* as much as by what is *included*. In addition to exploring what *is* in the story, ask what reasonably *could* be in the story (or, perhaps, even what *should* be in the story) but is *not* in the story. Similarly, characters and plots can be constructed as much by what they are *not* as by what they *are*. Story contents that serve to distance the story plot or characters from other kinds of plots or characters therefore are important. What is ignored? What is invisible? In what ways and with what consequences are story silences and exclusions patterned?

In summary, while examining data to answer explicit study questions is the goal of *all* research of *any* variety, story meaning always and necessarily is multiply contextualized so narrative analysis must include contextualizing storied data within the environment of their production as well as contextualizing particular research questions about stories within general story characteristics. While qualitative analysis *might* explicitly attend to various questions about context, narrative analysis *must* attend to these questions.

COMMUNICATING NARRATIVE RESEARCH

Because the field of narrative research is both new as well as an object of interest in multiple disciplines and professional fields, there is a lack of agreement about what this research should be as well as about how it should be done. In consequence, it rarely is possible for researchers to simply cite particular authorities to justify analytic decisions and procedures. Yet, if research is to be evaluated by relatively large audiences as sound with findings therefore worthy of attention, researchers must convince their audiences that the research design was logical and the data analytic techniques were systematic.

What does this mean to the practice of communicating research to others? As with all qualitative research, the evaluation of narrative research rests upon *persuasive communication*. While different audiences approach their reading of research with different expectations, what is universal is that arguments must be logical and examples must be of sufficient quantity and quality to be convincing. Because academic journals typically limit manuscripts to a specific number of pages, rarely can researchers relay to their audiences the multiple specific steps in the research process, all insights obtained from repeated rounds of close reading and data categorization, or all insights from asking questions about contextualization. Make choices carefully about what to present to audiences because each decision about what to present simultaneously is a decision about what not to present. My experience has been that it is not always or even often useful to consult a methods text for a "list" of what to cover in methods sections. Generic lists tend to miss what is important about a particular project offered to a particular audience. Rather, begin with images of audiences for the research: What kinds of issues about the research are likely of interest to those in intended audiences? Think also about likely audience reactions to different research elements: Are there likely questions about the appropriateness of the stories examined to answer particular study questions? Are there important implications from decisions about what stories to include/exclude? Do researcher characteristics raise particular questions about abilities to offer an analysis that is true to the data? This process of thinking through likely audience questions and reactions will lead to covering what needs to be covered for a particular project offered to a particular audience.

***

Chapters 3 and 4 have focused on some general principles of narrative as a social research method. The final chapters will offer empirical demonstrations of using narrative methods to explore questions about narrative productions of meaning.

NOTES

1. My focus on general principles of data analysis means I will not attend to specific topics such as special considerations when social media or websites are data, particular issues involved in particular kinds of data (such as social media, testimony from public policy hearings), the benefits and limitations of qualitative data software, and so on. Such specific topics rest upon general principles, and it is these general principles that are my interest here.

2. The exception is stories in the social problems genre which are crafted for the purpose of convincing disbelieving audiences that a problem exists that must be resolved. This story genre is characterized by a lack of ambiguity or complexity. It features characters who are pure victims or evil villains, and events that most certainly are morally intolerable.

3. In practice, the limited number of pages in journal manuscripts most often confines researchers to examining how meaning in a particular collection of stories is based on logical *or* emotional *or* moral evaluations. Larger projects could compare two or three types of meaning creation. It also is good practice to alert readers that analysts were paying particular attention to one or another of story appeal and not attending to others.

4. Comprehensive overviews of various ways to approach qualitative methods include Wertz et al.'s (2011) *Five Ways of Doing Qualitative Analysis: Phenomenological Psychology, Grounded Theory, Discourse Analysis, Narrative Research, and Intuitive Inquiry* and Gubrium and Holstein's (1997) *The New Language of Qualitative Method.* An overview of methods focusing on types of narrative analysis is Holstein and Gubrium's (2012) *Varieties of Narrative Analysis* and Riessman's (2008) *Narrative Methods for the Human Sciences.* Parts of the following discussion are adapted from Loseke (2012).

5. While the concept of "stance" is similar to that of "standpoint," stance is somewhat more general than standpoint which most often refers primarily or solely to social position/positions. Descriptions of various kinds of readings are found in Hall (1980) and Barthes (1982).

6. Data produced through a literal reading can be used to support conclusions that are distinctly critical. Additionally, doing two or more readings of the same storied data can yield important insights. See Loseke and Fawcett (1995) for an example.

7. The concept of data *categorization* should not be confused with the concept of data *coding.* True, the data *categorization* associated with constructionist informed research is similar to the data *coding* associated with naturalist inspired research in that both are about organizing data. Yet the two practices are dissimilar in fundamental ways: Data coding most often is a deductive process beginning with a codebook containing predetermined categories while data categorization is an inductive process with categories emerging from the data. Further, data coding typically is in the service of translating words into numbers amendable for quantitative analysis while data categorization retains the verbal qualities of data with a goal of organizing data into conceptual categories.

8. Zerubavel (1996) calls categorization the process of "lumping" and "splitting."

NARRATIVE
AS RESEARCH
PRACTICE

5 THE STORY CHARACTER OF THE "DESERVING POOR"

I will use the "Deserving Poor" story character to demonstrate the researchers' tasks of (1) forming research questions; (2) data and sampling decisions; (3) contextualizing data; (4) data categorization; and (5) communicating findings and their importance.[1]

FORMING RESEARCH QUESTIONS

My dissertation was an ethnography of a shelter for women who had been assaulted by their male partners. One of my most central findings was that workers had an image of a type of person (then called a "battered woman," now called a "victim of intimate partner violence") that they used as a yardstick to evaluate the characteristics of clients and potential clients. Simply put, women who fit their image of a battered woman type of person received shelter and worker support. Those who did not could be turned away.

According to how workers reacted to women and their stories, the experience of abuse was not sufficient to be evaluated as deserving of shelter and support. As I was trying to make sense of these findings, I became familiar with the work of Candace Clark (1997) who was exploring the cultural conventions surrounding the emotion of sympathy. Her research demonstrated a person was "sympathy worthy" when evaluated as (1) a good person, (2) greatly harmed, (3) through no fault. This seemed to fit my data. Women could tell workers about the abuse they experienced yet if workers evaluated these women as themselves aggressive, or as more angry than worried, if they did not seem to be good mother (and on and on), workers would categorize them as "not a battered woman" and deny them shelter and support. My initial interests were comparative: I wondered if what I found at the shelter was something about this particular organization, something about the battered woman as a particular type of character, or an example of a general social process of evaluating "sympathy worthiness."

Clark (1997) often demonstrated the components of evaluations of sympathy-worthiness with the example of the "deserving poor" narrative character constructed through the *New York Times* (*NYT*) newspaper yearly

"Neediest Cases" charity appeals. I decided to look more closely at these campaigns to see if they might offer data that seemed relevant for pursuing my interests.

DATA AND SAMPLING DECISIONS[2]

The first *NYT* Neediest Cases appeal was in 1912 and they continue yearly to the present. I started retrieving the text for the 1912 campaign and proceeded to do this for each subsequent year. Yet by the time I got to 1917 I had over 50 pages of data. Continuing to do this for each campaign to the present would have yielded thousands of pages of data—an amount most certainly not capable of being examined via narrative methodologies. More important was that close reading of these data showed major differences in the stories of the neediest over time. For example, the horrendous *physical* need in the first part of the twentieth century gradually became transformed to *psychological* distress; the depression of the 1930s greatly changed the content of appeals, as did the development of government programs of social welfare, and so on. Close reading convinced me that historical changes could not be ignored in understanding the evaluations of sympathy-worthiness. I needed a sample of a small number of years.

During initial close readings, I was most drawn to the early years of these campaigns which began on Thanksgiving with printing 100 stories *NYT* editors said were the neediest cases officially certified as requiring and deserving of readers' sympathy and charitable contributions. I have included the first 10 of these cases in the 1912 campaign at the end of this chapter.

I found these early campaigns particularly interesting because editors then *explicitly* directed their readers to feel sympathy for, and offer monetary support to, a type of person *they* called the "deserving poor." I decided to focus on the five earliest campaigns, 1912–1917. My justification was that this yielded an amount of data that was sufficient yet not overwhelming; a five-year span made it not necessary to empirically examine relationships between stories and social change. I further reasoned that using these early campaigns would allow me to empirically compare both types of people (deserving poor/battered women) and similarities/differences in evaluations of sympathy-worthiness over almost a century of time (*NYT* appeals at the beginning of the twentieth century and shelter work at the end of the century).

Sampling decisions of any type have consequences. In this case, my decision served to locate this study in history; I would not be able to make any empirically supported statements about the narrative character of the "deserving poor" in the present (yet see Chapter 6 for how one research project can lead to another).

CONTEXTUALIZING DATA

The first task of analysis is contextualization. While different sorts of stories will pose different contextualizing issues, most important for understanding the meaning of data for this study is: Who is the story author? Who is the intended audience? What is the story purpose? What is the social context of these campaigns?

Story authorship: Most certainly, the people described in the cases presented by the *NYT* did *not* author these stories themselves. Rather, story content was the product of a social process starting when social workers visited the homes of poor people in order to determine their need and assess their "worthiness" for assistance. Notes written by these workers were reviewed by their supervisors who decided which cases to submit to the *NYT*; an *NYT* employee wrote the story printed in the newspaper. This means it is *not possible* to know the extent to which the flesh and blood people represented by these stories would agree or disagree with what was written about them; it is *not possible* to judge the extent to which these stories might have exaggerated the consequences of poverty (in order to encourage donations) or discounted problems because stories were short and included few details of lives as they were lived. In consequence, these stories tell us *nothing* about poverty or the lives of poor people.

Story intended audience: The target story audience were readers of the *NYT*. Compared to the population in general, *NYT* readers—then and now—are English speaking and tend to be somewhat highly educated with upper-middle to upper levels of income. This means the criteria for what it took to be evaluated as the "deserving poor" (as opposed to the "undeserving poor") were *upper-middle- and upper-class criteria.*

Story purpose: The Neediest Cases charity appeals had three *explicit* purposes restated several times each and every year: To (1) encourage readers to donate money to specific charities working with the *NYT*, (2) educate readers about the characteristics of a type of person called the "deserving poor," and (3) educate readers about the characteristics and importance of an emerging new institution called "modern charity." As such, we would expect narrative characters—those defined as certified as charity-worthy—to be the type of person likely evaluated as deserving of readers' sympathy and support. This is why these campaigns furnished excellent data for my interest in the cultural meanings surrounding "sympathy-worthiness."

Social context: While contextualization of all stories is multidimensional (including social, political, historical), what is most important is that the 1912–1917 *NYT* Neediest Cases campaigns were located in an era with *no* publicly sponsored social support for poor people. In consequence, being evaluated by charity as "worthy" of assistance could lead to food, clothing, and medical help. Hence, while some observers might argue these stories are not important because they cannot be interpreted as a "truthful" rendition of the lives of poor people, editors regularly printed letters from readers describing how the stories in general or one story in particular led them to make a charitable donation. Stories encouraged readers to donate money; money bought food, fuel, and medicine; donations could be the difference between life and death.

DATA CATEGORIZATION

In order to categorize data, researchers must first decide *what* should be categorized and then *how* it should be categorized. In this instance, I began with my emotional reaction to the data.

As I read and reread the hundreds of stories and the accompanying comments from *NYT* editors and readers, my first reactions were strong and emotional: The horrors of poverty in the early 1900s! These folks would literally die if not helped: They were unable to get warm clothing to survive the New York winter (case 6); their lives were lived in a frenzy of fear (case 2); they were haggard for want of food and warm clothing (case 3); they suffered unknowable tortures (case 7). Further, as I read and reread the data I realized that my *own* reactions were very much in keeping with how *NYT* editors instructed their readers to evaluate these stories well over a century ago: These were people who *deserved* to be helped. And that, of course, is the question: What characteristics shared by story characters could be associated with the evaluation of their sympathy-worthiness?

My interest was in the concept of sympathy-worthiness and I knew that this is an outcome of a series of evaluations: A sympathy-worthy person is one evaluated as a good person, greatly harmed, through no fault. I felt I needed to give little attention to the component of "greatly harmed" given the life-threatening circumstances in these stories. So, too, understanding how an evaluation that story characters were not responsible for their plights seemed straightforward because most stories included the cause of dire need, and, *without exception*, these causes could not be evaluated as under individual control. Dire need was created by *illness* (tuberculosis in cases 1 and 8, leprosy in case 4), *disability* (blindness in case 2, semi-invalid in case 5), or *injury* (cases 3 and 7).

What was left to examine was how story characters were constructed in ways encouraging audience members to evaluate them as "good people." As a Sociologist, my first inclination was to look at demographic characteristics: How many of the characters were women/men; how many were married/single/widowed; children/adults/elderly; and so on? It did not take me long to realize that, while demographics certainly were important (the majority of donations were requested for narrative characters who were either very young or very old), simple *counts* of demographic characteristics were not particularly interesting. Upon reflection, this makes sense because demographic characteristics in and of themselves do not yield an image of a character who is—or who is not—evaluated as a "good person."

As is the case in many (if not most) narrative projects, what I should categorize in order to understand what characteristics led to an evaluation of "good person" was not obvious, and I spent considerable time pursuing topics which turned out to be not central in understanding the target concept of sympathy-worthiness. While at the time this was frustrating as I struggled to make sense of the data, in retrospect this was *not* time wasted. On the contrary, each failed categorization made me think about what was *not* apparently a component of the evaluation of sympathy-worthiness. My failed categorization systems, in other words, were the process of elimination of elements of evaluations of a "good person."

As I continued trying different forms of categorization, I gradually saw an underlying principle: These stories centered on how story characters could be evaluated as deserving of sympathy and support *as that evaluation could be made through middle-class understandings of culturally central systems of meaning in the early 1900s.*

First, important systems of meaning surrounding individualism and capitalism lead to beliefs that, if physically possible, people *should* work. Those who do this are evaluated as good people.

There is no doubt that the deserving poor are workers. These people work *incredibly* hard: Mom works almost day and night (case 1); mom is going blind but works in a brush factory (case 2); a 14-year-old is working "over hours" at a department store (case 3); Mrs. T does laundry although she has to take her children to the hospital daily (case 6); Mr. P was injured at work but "drags through" the pain of helping his wife with janitorial work (case 7); Mrs. D. works steadily and monstrously long hours (case 8); mom spends all her time and strength on her work (case 10). There are *no* people—not even one in any of the 200 stories in the actual sample—described as lazy or otherwise irresponsible. From time to time, cases did include a family member who was not exemplary. In each and every such case, stories explicitly included a statement that this member would not be receiving assistance (the husband in case 8 had deserted his family; the abusive husband in case 9 is in prison).

Additionally, the nonemployment of *children* is accounted for: The "eldest child, a little girl of 10, is, besides being far too young to earn any money, a helpless cripple" (case 4); One child, "in point of years able to work," was pronounced incurably deficient mentally (case 5); the "eldest child is only 5 years old" (case 6); Mrs. D is the mother of four babies, "all of them too young to help her" (case 8); the "eldest child is only 13 years old so that one more year stands between the little family and the faintest hope of any self-support" (case 10).

The deserving poor work incredibly hard yet, by definition, they fail to be self-sufficient. Establishing sympathy-worthiness therefore depends on establishing a "good reason" for a lack of self-sufficiency. Notably, the plot of *each* and *every* story contains an account for why the adults in the household were unable to be economically self-supporting. Adult characters suffer from: Insanity (case 1); blindness (case 2); injury which leads to being "helplessly bedridden" (case 3); leprosy (case 4); semi-invalid (case 5); "physical and mental distress" (case 7); tuberculosis (case 8).

Categorizations such as these soundly supported the argument that a "good person" is one who is employed. Additionally, while in some ways opposed to the cultural meaning systems surrounding individualism, *family* is a second kind of cultural meaning system. Moral worth is accorded to those who meet family obligations.

Story characters work for the good of their families: The mother works almost day and night "to maintain the family intact" (case 1); Mrs. C is going blind but works to "keep up her little family" (case 2); Mrs. F is "trying to provide for her four children" (case 5); Mr. and Mrs. P are both suffering "unknowable tortures" but they won't go to the hospital and leave five children uncared for (case 7); Mrs. C works to "support her four little children" (case 10).

In summary, categorization is the process of looking at what stories share. As the process continues, researchers gradually move from specifics (as in each of the above) to generalities: What do these characteristics share? I named the concept that tied them all together *morality*. A good person is a moral person, as morality is measured by early 1900s middle-class systems of meaning valuing home and work.

Categorization then can become the work of *subcategorization*. In this case, once I decided that a central element in the "good person" component of sympathy-worthiness was morality, I started to look at how morality could be subdivided. Again, this was not obvious and I tried several systems that I discarded either because they were too general (and therefore added nothing) or too specific (and therefore added too much detail at the cost of losing sight of larger meanings). I finally settled on three types of morality describing the deserving poor character.

First there was a morality of *biography*: These people were not lifelong dependents. Stories contained histories of labor before an accident, illness, or other event making employment not possible. Second, there was a morality of *activity*: Without exception, *no* story included anything that could be understood as fun or relaxation. Characters were fully occupied in doing what was needed for their survival. Third, there is a morality of *motivation*: Even if unable to work, these people *wanted* to work. They hated their state of dependence, they hated their need for charity. These stories were very short so, not surprisingly, they did not author each family in each way. Rather, *each* and *every* family featured at least one of these forms of morality.

COMMUNICATING FINDINGS AND THEIR IMPORTANCE

Based on this work, I concluded that the story of the neediest as formed through the *NYT* 1912–1917 neediest cases charity appeals was *melodramatic* in form (problems are none other than life-threatening, efforts to survive are none other than heroic). Story characters were good people, greatly harmed, through no fault and rather felled by accident, disability, or illness. The story plot of the inherent goodness of characters coupled with the devastating nature of their troubles led to the story moral that the deserving poor both required and deserved readers' charitable contributions.

This offered an answer to my original comparative questions: Although the deserving poor character was constructed by the *NYT* in the early part of the twentieth century and the battered woman character appeared on the social scene almost a century later, these characters are similar in that, when evaluated through dominant class understandings of important cultural meaning systems, both are morally evaluated as a good person, greatly harmed, through no fault.

Stories achieving their persuasiveness through including elements of important cultural meaning systems are of *practical importance* because of their consequences. In this instance, only those evaluated as the "deserving poor" received editors' and readers' sympathy and support; only those evaluated as the "battered woman" received workers' sympathy and support. Systems of meaning (capitalism, individualism, family, etc.) incorporated into culturally circulating stories can become yardsticks to evaluate the morality of particular people and such evaluations can encourage social approval or social condemnation, which, in turn, justify the presence or absence of social assistance.

DATA

1912 *NYT* Neediest Cases

Tuberculosis Haunts Them: Case 1

The husband and father of the family is insane and is now an inmate in one of the State asylums. Two of the seven children are at Ottsville, victims of tuberculosis. A third, a boy of 11, is in St. Joseph's Hospital, receiving treatment for tuberculosis and still another, a little chap of 7, has recently developed the same disease and is waiting admission to Ottsville. There are three younger children, seemingly in fair health and they, with the afflicted boy of 7, are at home with their mother. The mother, herself exhausted and devitalized, works almost day and night to maintain the family intact, but she has never been able to make more than $5 a week. She is rapidly breaking down her own health and she is haunted by the fear that the younger children, deprived of their normal heritage of warmth and nourishment and shelter, will become tuberculosis patients at Ottsville.

Preparing for Blindness: Case 2

Mrs. C is a widow with two young children. She is almost totally blind. Knowing that absolute blindness was to be her final destiny, she has trained herself at brush making, which she will be able to do when her sight is entirely gone. She works in a brush factory, earning $5 a week and with this she tries to keep up her little family. The two children are almost uncannily self-reliant, but they, as well as the mother, dread the day of her blindness with a kind of stupefied terror. This specter has so overshadowed and devitalized them that they are prey to nervous diseases and within the year just past the half-blind little mother has spent her nights groping feebly to the task of nursing them, her days in a frenzy of fear that they will be dead before she can get back to them.

Child Keeping a Family: Case 3

Mr. W is a longshoreman, who, within the month, was injured at his work so that he is helplessly bedridden. He is the father of nine children, two of whom have St. Vitus' dance. All of them are haggard for want of food and warm clothing. The oldest of this pitiful little group is a few months past the legal working age and she is employed in a department store as cash girl. Her pittance is the only support of the nine babies and the injured father. She is now working over hours, tying up Christmas parcels.

A Crippled Girl at Work: Case 4

Minus even the miserable alleviation of a tiny salary, the family of Mr. and Mrs. N face Christmas this year. They are Armenian by birth, and were prospering after a modest fashion in the land of their adoption when less than a year ago it was learned that

Mr. N was suffering from leprosy. He was sent at once to a hospital and the grief of the mother so impaired her health, already failing, that she became an invalid. The eldest child, a little girl of 10, is, besides being far too young to earn any money, a helpless cripple. She cannot even move about the house. The giant problems of food and shelter devolve upon two younger children, the smallest a mite scarcely able to walk.

Providing for Four Children: Case 5

Mrs. F, a semi-invalid, is trying to provide for four children and herself on absolutely nothing. Four months ago her husband dropped dead at his work. There was no insurance, of course. The eldest child, in point of years able to work, was pronounced incurably deficient mentally, this child must be cared for constantly, and the burden falls equally upon the mother and the three younger children.

Small Business Wrecked: Case 6

Mrs. T is recently widowed, and she is trying to maintain herself and four babies on the $2.50 a week she earns by taking in laundry. They live in a single room in a basement. Mr. T and his wife, after years of conscientious saving, accumulated a little fund a short time ago with which they started a small restaurant. The terrific labor of caring for the place reduced the man's already insufficient vitality, and he sickened and died. The place was sold for a trifling sum, barely enough to bring into the world the baby who came after her father's death. The eldest child is only 5 years old and is in such a weakened physical condition that both she and her mother are obliged to go daily for dispensary treatment. It is between these visits that Mrs. T does her laundering. They have been unable to get any warm clothing this winter.

Unable to Have Operation: Case 7

Mr. and Mrs. P are both in tremendous physical and mental distress. Mr. P was injured by a fall through a hatchway in the factory where he worked and, as the fault was shown to be in no way traceable to the company for which he worked, he received no damages. After a short stay in the hospital, he came back to help his wife with her janitor work. The hospital surgeons told him that he would never recover till he had an operation but he persisted in going to his wife, and now both of them drag through their painful existences, suffering unknowable tortures sooner than take their pitiable bodies to a hospital and leave their five little children uncared for. Because of the cruel privations of their lives, these children are developing diseases that overshadow even the great bodily pain of their mother and father.

Mother With Tuberculosis: Case 8

Mrs. D is the mother of four babies, all of them too young to help her. Her husband deserted her two years ago and she has been unable to find any trace of him. After the shock of the first few weeks she worked so steadily and for such monstrously long hours that she developed tuberculosis. She is now in the hospital undergoing treatment. Her poor little family is so devitalized that the task of resisting disease is herculean. The children are now receiving help from the organization.

Father in Prison: Case 9

Fighting against the most excruciating want, little Mrs. F is trying to bring up her five children on the $5 a week earned by her oldest child. The father has been sent to prison for brutally mistreating his wife and children. Many of them still bear the scars of his cruelty. There is a baby less than a year old. Mrs. F. is extremely delicate. Many of the babies are in frail health and have to make frequent journeys to a hospital dispensary.

Deserted by Husband: Case 10

Mrs. C was deserted by her husband ten months ago and she went to work in a factory to support her four little children. Even with spending all her time and strength on her work, she could not devise any adequate maintenance for the babies and one after another of them grew weak and ailing and finally Mrs. C. lost her own health and had to leave the factory. The eldest child is only 13 years old, so that one more year stands between the little family and the faintest hope of any self-support. The mother will not be able to do outside work anymore.

NOTES

1. A more theoretically and empirically complete and complex version of this chapter was published in the *Sociological Quarterly* as "Appealing Appeals: Constructing Moral Worthiness, 1912–1917" (Loseke and Fawcett 1995).
2. Researchers can find data for all Neediest Cases appeals through the website of the *New York Times* Historical Archive. *NYT* nonsubscribers have free, unlimited access to articles printed before 1923 and after 1980. There are costs to download other articles. (https://archive.nytimes.com/www.nytimes.com/ref/membercenter/nytarchive.html).

6

THE STORY OF THE "AMERICAN DREAM"

I will use the example of the American Dream story to illustrate the analytic work of (1) forming research questions; (2) data and sampling decisions; (3) data categorization; (4) finding a story in data that are not in storied form; and (5) communicating findings and their importance.[1]

FORMING RESEARCH QUESTIONS

My interest in how the *New York Times* neediest cases data told the story of the "deserving poor" at the beginning of the twentieth century led me to be sensitive to how, by the mid-1990s, there was considerable public concern and anger toward programs of social welfare and their beneficiary, often referred to as the "welfare queen," a type of person whose behaviors of producing children with neither a husband nor the means for economic independence were evaluated by middle-class taxpayers as both immoral and a drain on public resources. The parallels seemed obvious between the story of the "deserving poor" evaluated as morally *worthy* and therefore deserving of sympathy and assistance and the "welfare queen" evaluated as morally *unworthy* and therefore undeserving of sympathy and assistance.

During the 1990s I also became interested in practical questions about what stories do in social life, and this led me to be attentive to the social processes surrounding federal welfare reform legislation called the Personal Responsibility and Work Opportunity Reconciliation Act (PRWORA). Reflecting taxpayer anger toward both the cost of welfare and its disliked beneficiaries, the proposed legislation greatly reduced benefits for poor women with children while increasing the requirements necessary to obtain assistance. My initial question was about how story characters (in this case, the "welfare queen") could justify the public policy (in this case, welfare reform): To what extent does the public image of the "welfare queen" story character justify the characteristics of social welfare policy?

Given this question, transcripts of federal public policy hearings seemed a logical source for data.

DATA AND SAMPLING DECISIONS

Hearings about social welfare policy reform were conducted in both the United States Senate and the House. Because the proposed legislation was comprehensive (including programs of cash support, food, housing, childcare, medical care, education), these hearings were held by many committees and subcommittees (such as Ways and Means, Economic and Educational Opportunities, Governmental Affairs, Agriculture, Education, Labor and Human Resources, Finance, and Agriculture, Nutrition and Forestry). In all, there were over 60 hearings together producing several thousand pages of text.[2]

It was clear in close readings that the welfare queen character was critical in supporting the need for welfare reform: Repeated testimonies justified reform as necessary because current policy encouraged irresponsibility by offering public support to women who acted irresponsibly. Indeed, I began to wonder if an empirical analysis would be quite boring because the importance of this character was so obvious. Further, research on welfare reform policy had been appearing regularly in journals of social policy and sociology and this, too, often linked public condemnation of the welfare queen with policies of benefit reduction. I decided to abandon the project because it seemed neither new nor interesting.

Merely to satisfy my curiosity about how legislative attention had ended, I decided to read the final hearing of House of Representatives.[3] This hearing took place *after* it was known that the bill would pass in both the House and Senate; participants also knew that then-President Clinton would sign it. Not surprisingly, this hearing differed from all others leading to the legislation. In *form*, while called a "hearing," there was no dialogue or debate. Rather, this was a rapid progression of 81 speakers, each given only a minute or two to talk. In *content*, this hearing primarily contained legislators' reasons why they were about to vote for or against the legislation. This hearing, therefore, was the formal occasion for members of the House of Representatives to go on the *official record* with their justifications for supporting or opposing the legislation.

While I abandoned my initial focus on the welfare queen character, I decided this particular hearing was important data that deserved empirical examination. The hearing differed in *purpose* from the many hearings leading to the shape of welfare reform; it differed in both *form* and *content* from other hearings; it had not been the topic of academic attention. Further, and most important, it allowed me to ask new questions about stories in social policy: Rather than simply noting *that* stories are a common speech form in social policy, this hearing allowed exploring *how* stories could be used to justify political decision-making. So, my research question changed from one about the welfare queen character as justification for social policy to a more general question about the extent to which stories can serve to justify social policy.

The benefits of using testimonies in this hearing as data were accompanied by costs. In particular, I could *not* use it to examine the kinds of arguments and debates that shaped the policy. This was unfortunate because close reading made it obvious that the content of this hearing was far different from the content of others. Most notably, the despised "welfare queen" character, a recurring component in many hearings, as well as much examined in social research, was all but absent in this final hearing. Likewise, while earlier hearings often contained racist assumptions reflecting public misconceptions that "unmarried, poor mothers" were primarily African American women, race was *not* mentioned in the final hearing. Such differences were quite predictable: Despite their central importance in decision-making, political decision-making cannot be justified by emotion or prejudice. On the record, policy must be *morally justified* in terms relatively congruent with voters' understandings of the ways the world works and the ways the world should work.

DATA CATEGORIZATION

I have included three of the 81 testimonies at the end of this chapter. These examples offer clear demonstrations that the policy hearing itself was *not* in the form of a story and that these data could be used to examine several topics of interest to social researchers exploring questions other than those of narrative productions of meaning. For example, testimonies could be used to explore differences between Republicans' and Democrats' understanding of poverty and programs of social welfare; to examine how the perceived needs and desires of taxpayers justify policy change; to enumerate the perceived problems with the current system of social welfare. Each of these—and many others—could be excellent topics for social research that could be examined with these particular data.

As always the case, researchers' interests inform how data are read and interpreted. In this instance, my attention was focused on stories and political justification, so my orientation to reading this transcript was through the lens of narrative. It was repeated close readings that led me to notice how the story of the "American Dream" wove its way through the testimonies of both those who supported the legislation as well as those who opposed it.

I do not need to say much about the contents of the American Dream story because, although observers often argue it is an untruthful rendition of opportunities in the United States, they simultaneously note how widely known and deeply embraced this story is throughout the general population. In shorthand form, the *setting* of the story is the United States, assumed to be a place of endless opportunities allowing widespread economic and social mobility. This is a *character-driven* story featuring the "good American" character distinguished by behavior (endless activity), motivation (desire to be self-reliant), and psychological disposition (meeting obstacles with resolve and optimism). The *plot* of the story is that such hard work eventually yields a happy ending of success as measured in terms of money, social standing, and family well-being. The story *morals* are that success is achieved through individual labor; individuals wanting to achieve success must do the hard work necessary to take advantage of opportunities; diligence is rewarded.

While there have been multiple changes in the meanings of the American Dream story over time, what does not change is that this is the storied form of a set of widely held and deeply embraced cultural codes: Individualism (the values of self-determination and self-responsibility), capitalism (the values of work and private profit), fair play (the value of equality of opportunity), meritocracy (the value of rewards based on individual achievement), and family (the value of attachment to, and responsibility for, a particular set of others).[4]

My data categorization therefore was *deductive*. I began with understandings of the characteristics of the American Dream story (a topic of countless books and articles) and looked for components of the story in the transcript.

FINDING A STORY IN NONSTORIED DATA

The story of the American Dream was *explicitly* referenced by 12 of the 81 legislators who spoke in this final hearing on welfare policy reform. Such direct referencing was primarily used to justify the need to change the current system evaluated as preventing Americans from achieving the Dream. Some examples include:

> *Today's welfare system…* "*robs human beings of hope and life and any opportunities at the American Dream*"
>
> (Cunningham, R-California)

[we must] offer poor families "a new chance for a better life and an opportunity to participate in the American dream".

(Franks, D-Connecticut)

The particular set of values associated with the American Dream story (work and family are valued while dependency is devalued) are repeated throughout testimonies to criticize the current system of welfare:

Mr. Speaker, the American welfare system was intended to be a safety net for those who fall on hard times. Unfortunately, it has become an overgrown bureaucracy which perpetuates dependency and denies people the chance to live the American dream.

(Fowler, R-Florida)

I strongly believe in the American dream where each individual is given the opportunity to work, provide for their family, and participate in our society. The current welfare system has taken that dream away from too many Americans.

(Goodlatte, R-Virginia)

Because the purpose of this hearing was to allow legislators to justify their votes, it is not surprising that there is repeated and explicit talk of values. Legislators talked of how reform must be based on "fundamental American values" (Kasich, R-Ohio), and these values—enclosed within the American Dream story—were explicitly defined. Chief among these were those associated with individualism:

We need to "move toward a system that better promotes work and individual responsibility".

(Stenholm, D-Texas)

We must "promot[e] self-sufficiency versus creating an expectation of dependence"

(Hayes, D/R-Louisiana)

Such self-responsibility was said to be necessary for individual well-being:

[what we ought to emphasize is a system] that would allow poor people to achieve "a sense of self-worth inherent in work"

(Moakley, D-Massachusetts)

...an "increased sense of self-worth that necessarily comes with a pay check"

(Goodlatte, R-Virginia H9421)

Another value associated with the American Dream story, the importance of family, also was prominent in legislator's justifications for their votes. According to them, welfare reform was about:

[s]trengthening families and instilling personal responsibility

(Hoyer, D-Maryland)

"saving families" rather than "breaking them"

(Tanner, D-Tennessee H9419)

promoting the "enduring strength of families rather than promoting dependency and illegitimacy"

(Pryce, R-Ohio)

Finally, legislators were clear in describing the characteristics of people who should be helped by programs of welfare which, simultaneously, produced the categories of people who should *not* be helped. Simply stated, who should be helped were those evaluated as exemplars of the "good American" character:

Americans are a compassionate people, eager to lend a helping hand to hard workers experiencing temporary difficulties and especially to children who are victims of circumstances beyond their control

(Tanner, D-Tennessee)

We must help those struggling who "through no fault of their own, must turn to their Government for help in times of need"

(Clay, D-Missouri)

[G]overnments should help people who are too sick, too old or too young to help themselves

(Sabo, D-Minnesota)

In summary, my categorization of these data was deductive: I began with images of the American Dream story and looked for instances of those components in testimonies. The analytic work was that of finding segments of testimonies that could be categorized as instances of one or another component (setting, plot, character, moral) of the American Dream story. In the process, I transformed testimony that was not in storied form into a story, a story about how the story of the American Dream justified political decision-making.

COMMUNICATING FINDINGS AND THEIR IMPORTANCE

This project demonstrates how elements of widely known and deeply embraced cultural meaning systems (in this case, democracy, individualism, capitalism, fair play, meritocracy, family) incorporated into stories (in this case, the American Dream) can be used as powerful *moral* justifications for decisions (in this case, political decisions surrounding social policy). Those supporting the new policy as well as those opposing it were united in criticizing the then-current social welfare system as hindering poor people's chances of achieving the American Dream. In turn, those opposing the new policy did so on grounds it would continue to prevent poor people from achieving the American Dream while those supporting the policy did so on grounds it would encourage poor people to achieve the dream. Those supporting the policy were successful, and the policy was approved with the justification that it would be good for poor people despite the fact that, in reality, it would greatly decrease the social support offered to poor women and their children.

The American Dream is a lovely story containing images of unlimited opportunities rather than the empirically verifiable racial, gendered, and class inequalities structured into American social and economic institutions. As such, the American Dream story makes invisible the inconvenient facts of life in a social order that can make it difficult, if not all but impossible, for poor people to achieve the dream that the story promises. Such is the power of stories used as justification for political decision-making.

DATA

Mr. LONGLEY. Mr. Speaker, I want to compliment the gentleman from New York [Mr. Solomon], chair of the Committee on Rules, and also members of the committee for bringing this important legislation to the floor. This has been delayed far too long. This is a bill that is about child abuse. It is drug abuse. It is crime and violence and the fact that, for too many Americans who are trapped in this system, the American dream has become the American nightmare. I do not argue with the fact that the welfare system is a hand in need to those who need it. But for too many it has become a prison. This is about women and children who are suffering under this system as well as the social workers and the law enforcement officers who are forced to deal with the ramifications of the aspects of the system that do not work. Mr. Speaker, for too long we have been delaying this. We have delayed this vote for most of the day. The fact of the matter is that welfare reform is at the door. It has been knocking for almost 30 years, and it is finally here today. This afternoon, hopefully, it will be voted on and we will send it to a President who will endorse it. I think that is a tremendous accomplishment for the people of this country. I would also say it is a first step. The system has become so complex between the different aspects of service and how they are available to help people, that even the people running the system have difficulty understanding it, let alone those who have need for assistance. So, it is a first step in the direction of reform, in the direction of providing an American dream for more Americans and getting rid of the American nightmare.

Mr. KINGSTON. Mr. Speaker, I thank the gentleman from New York for yielding. It is interesting we have heard from the Democrats a number reasons why they are not going to support this bill today. One of their reasons was they have not had time to look at it. I am a relatively new Member of Congress. I have been here 4 years. We have been debating welfare for 4 years. I know that for a fact. I have been here. If they have not read the bill by now and have not been following the debate, that is not the fault of the Republican Congress. The second reason they say that is that welfare does not cost that much. If you add in all the Federal Government welfare programs, the cost is $345 billion, which is more than we spend on defense. I am not sure what they consider money if $345 billion is not. We spent $5 trillion since LBJ's Great Society programs, and that is enough money. That is more than we spent on World War II. The final reason they are saying is that it is cruel to children. Nothing is more cruel than having a welfare system that traps children in poverty, that makes children and families break up, that makes them live in housing projects where the dad cannot be at home, where there is high drug use, where there are teenage dropout rates and teenage drug abuse. I do not see why they think that is compassion. Our program sends $4 billion more on child care than the Democrat proposal. And that is using their frame of thinking that is more compassion than what they have. Welfare reform is family friendly. Welfare should not be a life style. It should be something that society gives people a temporary helping hand, not a permanent handout, not a hammock forever to swing in but a temporary safety net so that people can get back into the socio-economic mainstream and enjoy the American dream just like the rest of us.

Mr. MANZULLO. Mr. Speaker, in the last 31 years this country has spent over $5.4 trillion on the welfare system, and what do we have to show for it? We have generation after generation locked in a seemingly endless cycle of destitution and poverty. They are the lost forgotten statistics, dependent on the Federal entitlement trap that strips them of their dignity, destroys families, damages our work ethic, and destroys the self-esteem of those trapped in the system. Cruelty is allowing this destructive system to continue. By passing this welfare reform bill we will restore hope and opportunity by making work, and not welfare, a way of life. Our current welfare system has not only failed those in the system, but it has also failed those who have been supporting it, the hard working taxpayer. It has failed the forgotten American, the one who gets up in the morning, packs a lunch, sends the kids off to school. That person is working harder than ever to make ends meet, and the typical American family is paying over $3,400 a year in taxes for welfare payments to perpetuate a failed system. Mr. Speaker, we should pass this bill and pass it swiftly.

NOTES

1. This chapter is an extended version of "Narrative Analysis of Documents: Social Policy Hearings and Welfare Reform" (D. Loseke and J. Beahm). *Sage Research Methods Datasets*, Thousand Oaks, CA: SAGE (2015).

2. Janine Beahm offered valuable assistance in finding and reading these transcripts.

3. The Pro-Quest Congressional data base marked the legislative hearings related to the "Responsibility and Work Opportunity Reconciliation Act" (PRO-WORA) as beginning in 1992 in the 102nd Congress and concluding in 1996, the 104th Congress. A pdf file of the proceedings used as data for this project can be found in the House Congressional Record for July 31, 1996. In original form, this is 32 pages of text (H9392–H9424), 147 pages when transformed to a searchable word file (CREC-1996-07-31-pt1-PgH9392.pdf (congress.gov)).

4. Social observers have shown considerable interest in understanding the contents, uses, and consequences of the American Dream story. See, for example, Loseke (2019), Rowland and Jones (2007), and Samuel (2012).

7

THE STORY
CHARACTER OF
THE "DREAMER"

My final example of the practices of narrative analysis, the story character of the Dreamer, is not taken from research I have done. Rather, I wanted a small amount of data that would demonstrate how narrative analysis can speak to issues of *immediate* and *practical* concern. With such data, I will focus on the analytic practices of (1) establishing story political and social contexts; (2) categorizing data; and (3) communicating findings and their importance.

ESTABLISHING POLITICAL AND SOCIAL CONTEXTS

Data for this example are from a United States Congressional Hearing titled "Dreamers Are Americans."[1] While there are many contexts surrounding the production and evaluation of stories of any kind, the most centrally important for these data are social and political.

Historically, there are two competing stories of immigration and immigrants in the United States—be they Chinese immigrants in the early mid-1800s, Irish immigrants in the early 1900s, or Latinx immigrants in the 2000s. One is the "good immigrant" story promoting the positive social and economic values of immigration and the virtue of those who immigrate to the United States. The other is the "bad immigrant" story emphasizing the harms of immigration and the immorality of those who immigrate.[2] As with the American Dream story (Chapter 6), these two versions of the immigration story can be used to justify decision-making.

This Congressional hearing took place in 2019, a time when then-President Donald Trump had been relentlessly and loudly promoting the "bad immigrant" story on public stages. For several years he had been encouraging American citizens to define immigrants as none other than evil people, bringing with them disease, crime, and immorality that would destroy the United States. This is the immediate social context of this hearing.

Social context leads to the political context. At the time of this hearing, United States Supreme Court judges were reviewing the President's plan to phase out DACA (Deferred Action for Childhood Arrivals). This is a federal immigration policy beginning with an executive branch memorandum signed by then-President Barack Obama on June 15, 2012, in response to the repeated failures of Congress to pass the Development, Relief, and Education Act for Alien Minors (DREAM Act). The DACA program offers undocumented immigrants who were brought to the United States as children the opportunity to defer their deportation and the ability to apply for work permits. Immigrants remaining in the United States because of DACA commonly are called "Dreamers."

Social and historical contexts combine to make this a hearing about a topic that is both immediate and practical. Simply put, should the DACA program be declared unconstitutional, millions of young people could find themselves without the ability to continue their education or to be employed. Indeed, it would raise the possibility of their deportation from the United States, the only country many of them had known as "home."

These social and political contexts also are associated with shaping the characteristics of this hearing in two related ways. First, immigration in 2019 was a highly partisan issue with Republicans overwhelmingly advancing the bad immigrant story and Democrats overwhelmingly advancing the good immigrant story. In this short hearing, all four Congressional members testifying were Democrats (I have included at the end of this chapter relevant segments of testimony of two of those who testified). As such, this hearing did *not* contain debate. Second, and related, the title of the hearing, "Dreamers are Americans," encourages audiences to categorize the Dreamer character as an American, not as a foreigner. In consequence, these data could not be used to talk about the immigration debate in the United States or in the House of Representatives; it could not be used to explore dimensions of the bad immigrant story.

CONTEXTUALIZING DATA

Researchers must decide both what to categorize as well as how to categorize it. As is typical—even when data are in the form of interviews conducted by the researcher—much of the available data will not be relevant to the particular research project being designed. In this case, presenters talked about a range of issues—the history and characteristics of the DACA program, the unfairness of the attacks from those opposing the program, program costs, program needs, and so on. Although each of these could be a very good topic of social research, my interest was in how these testimonies constructed images of a narrative character called the Dreamer. This hearing seemed a very appropriate source of data for such a project because the hearing title,

"Dreamers are Americans," would lead to expectations that testimony can be understood as creating a *character-driven* story.

DATA CATEGORIZATION

I have <u>underlined</u> explicit descriptions of the Dreamer character in the 36 lines of testimony I have included at the end of this chapter. In practice, I would make a word file of such descriptions and then try different ways to categorize them. While an actual research project would use considerably more data, and while individual researchers will notice different elements of descriptions in this text, here are some examples of insights and their supporting data (line numbers) from categorization.

First, and as stated explicitly by the hearing title, "Dreamers" are Americans. This is the only country they have ever known (lines 3–4); Dreamers are our friends…and neighbors (lines 6–7); Germain Martinez Garcia is part of this community (line 23). Indeed, not only are Dreamers Americans, they are exemplary because they reflect and represent…the American Dream (lines 9–10).

Second, the central theme in these testimonies is that "Dreamers" are instances of the socially valued "Good American" character (see previous chapter). For example, Dreamers are *not* rule-breakers: They are not responsible for their undocumented immigrant status because they came here through no choice of their own (line 3). Additionally, Dreamers are hard workers: They are in schools, in community colleges, and in the State Universities (lines 8–9). Hard work is exemplified by individual Dreamers: As an intern, his hard work and positive attitude…earned him a slot in the local [police]academy (lines 20–21); although his immigration status made it very difficult, Cesar Vargas was admitted to the New York State Bar (lines 27–28).

Furthermore, Dreamers are achievers: They have made immense contributions to our society every day (lines 5–6). For example, Cesar Vargas passed the New York bar on his first try (line 26); Germain Martinez Garcia is a valued member of his team and his department (line 22); Gloria Montiel received a master's degree from Harvard (line 35) and is a PhD candidate from Claremont Graduate University (line 36).

And, Dreamers are patriotic. They are patriotic in their behavior: Jose enlisted in the United States Marine Corps (line 16); Cesar served our Nation in the Army (line 25); John joined the US Army (line 30). Indeed, Dreamers make the ultimate sacrifice for the United States: Jose was deployed to Iraq and in 2003 was killed at the age of 21 (line 17). Likewise, they are patriotic in their motivation: John wants nothing more than to defend our country (line 31).

Notice how testimonies author the character of the Dreamer in two ways. At times, they author Dreamer as a particular type of person (statements using plural terms such as "Dreamers are" or "they are"). At other times, particular people are categorized as members of this category of person ("Cesar Vargas is a Dreamer," "Gloria Montiel is a Dreamer"). Dreamer is a type of character; specific people can be categorized as this character type.

Not uncommonly, what is *not* in a story can be as important as what *is* in the story. In this case, by legal definition, those who are Dreamers began life in a country other than the United States. Yet such origins are *not* a part of this character. The Dreamer is a character without a past. What is important are the character's present and future and these are—and should be—located in the United States. Second, notice how each and every attribute of the Dreamer (either as a general character or a specific person) typically receives positive evaluation among audiences of citizens of the United States. The Dreamer therefore is similar to both the "deserving poor" and the "good American" character in that each is morally evaluated as an exemplary person *as measured by the standards of dominant class citizens.*

COMMUNICATING FINDINGS AND THEIR IMPORTANCE

These 36 lines of Congressional testimony combine to author a type of character called the Dreamer, and they author specific people (Cesar, John, Gloria, etc.) as people of that type. Systems of meaning—cultural codes—associated with the story of the "American Dream" and the person of the "good American" (see previous chapter) are the building blocks for this construction. Authoring people in terms of the values displayed in the American Dream story encourages wide segments of the general population to evaluate "Dreamers" as truly "Americans" and therefore worthy of remaining in this country.

Stories have practical uses and they have practical consequences. In this instance, authoring the Dreamer as an exemplary American is a justification for supporting policies of their continued inclusion. In this particular case, when testimony is read in storied form it serves as a moral justification for maintaining a social policy allowing Dreamers to fully participate in American society. Yet because the character is exemplary in both behavior and motivation it sets a very high bar. The character of the Dreamer produces a yardstick by which to measure the "worthiness" of particular people. Are people who are evaluated as not so perfectly exemplary still Dreamers? Is their inclusion in the United States justified? The character of the Dreamer justifies policies of inclusion, yet the character justifies inclusion for only those who are exemplary in every way.

DATA

1 (Testimony of Jim Costa, D-California): Madam Speaker, I rise today to talk about an important issue
2 affecting our country, and that is Dreamers…Dreamers are Americans just like you and me, and they should
3 be treated as such. These Dreamers came here through no choice of their own, but for them, this is the only
4 country they have ever known. They were qualified and granted, under this program enacted by the Obama
5 administration, to be protected from deportation and, thus, granted a legal status. Since then, these young
6 people have made immense contributions to our society every day. They are our friends. They are our
7 neighbors. For 243 years, America has been a beacon of shining light for immigrants around the world…I
8 know these Dreamers. I have visited with them. They are in my schools, in the community colleges, and in
9 the State universities. And so I want them to know, I want you to know because these Dreamers reflect and
10 represent what? The American Dream. What is the American Dream? The American Dream is about
11 immigrants past and immigrants present, and it is the embodiment of what Dreamers are a part of.
12
13 (Testimony of Jose L. Correa D-California): I represent central Orange County, home to the largest number
14 of Dreamers in the United States. I will talk a little bit about a few of the Dreamers in my district.
15
16 The first one, Jose Angel Garibay…enlisted in the United States Marine Corps. Jose was deployed to Iraq,
17 and in 2003 he was killed at the age of 21. Jose was the first service member from Orange County to make
18 the ultimate sacrifice. Jose Angel Garibay, rest in peace. Jose is a Dreamer.
19
20 Police officer Germain Martinez Garcia grew up in southern Illinois. As an intern, his hard work and
21 positive attitude set him apart and earned him a slot in the local academy. Germain Martinez Garcia is a
22 valued member of his team and his department. In the words of his police chief: "He is part of this
23 community. He's a good citizen. He's a good person. We need him." Germain Martinez, a Dreamer.
24
25 Cesar Vargas grew up in Staten Island. He has served our Nation in the Army. After law school, Cesar
26 passed the New York bar on his first try. Then he applied for admission to the New York bar, but due to his
27 immigration status, he was denied. It would take him five more years before Cesar became the first Dreamer
28 admitted to the New York State bar. Cesar Vargas. He is a Dreamer.
29
30 John grew up in southern California. John joined the U.S. Army, and on March 18 of last year, he shipped
31 out to basic training. John wants nothing more than to defend our country. John is a warrior and a patriot.
32 John is a Dreamer.
33
34 Gloria Montiel is the first student from Santa Ana High School to be accepted to Harvard. Gloria was the
35 first undocumented student to receive a master's degree from Harvard. Gloria was the first undocumented
36 Ph.D. candidate from Claremont Graduate University. Gloria Montiel is a Dreamer.

NOTES

1. Data are from: "Dreamers are Americans" in the *Congressional Record*, Vol. 165, no. 181. November 13, 2019. HH8816–8820. The original was four pages of three-column print, 10 pages when translated to a single-spaced, one-column word document. (CREC-2019-11-13-pt1-PgH8816-3.pdf (congress.gov)).

2. The large and ever-expanding literature on images of immigration and immigrants in the United States includes Chavez (2008) and Edwards and Herder (2012).

REFERENCES

Aguirre, Adalberto, Jr., Edgar Rodriguez, and Jennifer K. Simmers. 2011. "The Cultural Production of Mexican Identity in the United States: An Examination of the Mexican Threat Narrative." *Social Identities* 17: 695–707.

Alcoff, Linda, and Laura Gray. 1993. "Survivor Discourse: Transgression or Recuperation?" *Signs: Journal of Women in Culture and Society* 18: 260–290.

Alexander, Jeffrey C. 2017. *The Drama of Social Life*. Malden, MA: Polity.

Alexander, Jeffrey C., and Philip Smith. 1993. "The Discourse of American Civil Society: A New Proposal for Cultural Studies." *Theory and Society* 22: 151–207.

Altheide, David L. 2002. *Creating Fear: News and the Construction of Crisis*. Hawthorne, NY: Aldine de Gruyter.

Amsterdam, Anthony G., and Jerome Bruner. 2000. *Minding the Law: How Courts Rely on Storytelling, and How Their Stories Change the Ways We Understand the Law—and Ourselves*. Cambridge, MA: Harvard University Press.

Andrews, Molly. 2019. "The Narrative Architecture of Political Forgiveness." *Political Psychology* 40: 289–314.

Aristotle. 1926. *The Art of Rhetoric*. Translated by J. H. Freese. Loeb Classical Library 195. Cambridge, MA: Harvard University Press.

Atkinson, Paul, and Sara Delamont. 2006. "Rescuing Narrative From Qualitative Research." *Narrative Inquiry* 16: 164–172.

Balch, Alex, and Ekaterina Balabanova. 2011. "A System in Chaos? Knowledge and Sense-making on Immigration Policy in Public Debates." *Media, Culture, & Society* 33: 885–904.

Barcelos, Christie A., and Aline C. Gubrium. 2014. "Reproducing Stories: Strategic Narratives of Teen Pregnancy and Motherhood." *Social Problems* 61: 466–481.

Barthes, Roland. 1982. *Mythologies*. New York, NY: Hill & Wang.

Barton, Ellen. 2007. "Disability Narratives of the Law: Narratives and Counter-Narratives." *Narrative* 15: 95–113.

Beck, Christina S., Stellina M. Aubuchon, Timothy P. McKenna, Stephanie Ruhl, and Nathaniel Simmons. 2014. "Blurring Personal Health and Public Priorities: An Analysis of Celebrity Health Narratives in the Public Sphere." *Health Communication* 29: 244–256.

Becker, Gay. 1997. *Disrupted Lives: How People Create Meaning in a Chaotic World*. Berkeley, CA: University of California Press.

Bell, Jill S. 2002. "Narrative Inquiry: More Than Just Telling Stories." *TESOL Quarterly* 36: 207–213.

Bellah, Robert N., Richard Madsen, William M. Sullivan, Ann Swidler, and Steven M. Tipton. 1985. *Habits of the Heart: Individualism and Commitment in American Life.* Berkeley, CA: University of California Press.

Berbrier, Mitch. 2000. "Ethnicity in the Making: Ethnicity Work, the Ethnicity Industry, and a Constructionist Framework for Research." In *Perspectives on Social Problems,* edited by James A. Holstein, and Gale Miller, vol. 12, 69–87. Greenwich, CT: JAI Press.

Berger, Arthur A. 1997. *Narratives in Popular Culture, Media, and Everyday Life.* Thousand Oaks, CA: SAGE.

Berger, Ronald J., and Richard Quinney. 2005. "The Narrative Turn in Social Inquiry." In *Storytelling Sociology: Narrative as Social Inquiry,* edited by Ronald J. Berger, and Richard Quinney, 1–12. Boulder, CO: Lynn Reiner.

Bergstrand, Kelly, and James M. Jasper. 2018. "Villains, Victims, and Heroes in Character Theory and Affect Control Theory." *Social Psychology Quarterly* 91: 228–247.

Best, Joel. 1997. "Victimization and the Victim Industry." *Society* 34: 9–17.

Bohmer, Carol, and Amy Schuman. 2018. *Political Asylum Deceptions: The Culture of Suspicion.* Cham: Palgrave Macmillan.

Boltanski, Luc. 1999. *Distant Suffering: Morality, Media and Politics.* Cambridge: Cambridge University Press.

Borland, Elizabeth. 2014. "Storytelling, Identity, and Strategy: Perceiving Shifting Obstacles in the Fight for Abortion Rights in Argentina." *Sociological Perspectives* 57: 488–505.

Boswell, Christina, Andrew Geddes, and Peter Scholten. 2011. "The Role of Narratives in Migration Policy-Making: A Research Framework." *British Journal of Politics and International Relations* 13: 1–11.

Brooks, Peter. 1976. *The Melodramatic Imagination: Balzac, Henry James, Melodrama, and the Mode of Excess.* New Haven, CT: Yale University Press.

Bruner, Jerome. 1987. "Life as Narrative." *Social Research* 54: 11–32.

Burchardt, Marian. 2016. "The Self as Capital in the Narrative Economy: How Biographical Testimonies Move Activism in the Global South." *Sociology of Health & Illness* 38: 592–609.

Burr, Vivien. 2015. *Social Constructionism,* 3rd ed. New York, NY: Routledge.

Cabaniss, Emily R. 2019. "Shifting the Power": Youth Activists' Narrative Reframing of the Immigrant Rights Movement." *Sociological Inquiry* 89: 482–507.

Calhoun, Craig, and Jonathan VanAntwerpen. 2007. "Orthodoxy, Heterodoxy, and Hierarchy: 'Mainstream' Sociology and Its Challengers." In *Sociology in America: A History,* edited by Craig Calhoun, 367–410. Chicago, IL: University of Chicago Press.

Casey, Briege, Denise Proudfoot, and Melissa Corbally. 2016. "Narrative in Nursing Research: An Overview of Three Approaches." *Journal of Advanced Nursing* 72: 1203–1215.

Cerulo, Karen A. 1998. *Deciphering Violence: The Cognitive Structure of Right and Wrong*. New York, NY: Routledge.

Chavez, Leo. 2008. *The Latino Threat: Constructing Immigrants, Citizens, and the Nation*. Stanford, CA: Stanford University Press.

Clark, Candace. 1997. *Misery and Company: Sympathy in Everyday Life*. Chicago, IL: University of Chicago Press.

Collins, Patricia H. 1989. "The Social Construction of Invisibility: Black Women's Poverty in Social Problems Discourse." In *Perspectives on Social Problems*, edited by James A. Holstein, and Gale Miller, vol. 1, 77–94. Greenwich, CT: JAI Press.

Crotty, Michael. 2015. *The Foundations of Social Research: Meaning and Perspective in the Research Process*. Thousand Oaks, CA: SAGE.

D'Andrade, Roy. 1995. *The Development of Cognitive Anthropology*. Cambridge: Cambridge University Press.

Davis, Joseph E. 2002. "Narrative and Social Movements: The Power of Stories." In *Stories of Change: Narrative and Social Movements*, edited by Joseph E. Davis, 3–30. Albany, NY: State University of New York Press.

DeCamp, Elise. 2017. "Negotiating Race in Stand-up Comedy: Interpretations of 'Single Story' Narratives." *Social Identities* 23: 326–342.

DeGloma, Thomas. 2014. *Seeing the Light: The Social Logic of Personal Discovery*. Chicago, IL: University of Chicago Press.

DiMaggio, Paul. 1997. "Culture and Cognition." *Annual Review of Sociology* 23: 263–287.

Dinerstein, Robert D. 2007. "Every Picture Tells a Story, Don't It?: The Complex Role of Narratives in Disability Cases." *Narrative* 15: 40–58.

Durkheim, Emile. 1961. *The Elementary Forms of Religious Life*. New York, NY: Macmillan.

Edwards, Jason A., and Richard Herder. 2012. "Melding a New Immigration Narrative? President George W. Bush and the Immigration Debate." *Howard Journal of Communications* 23: 40–65.

Emerson, Robert M. 1997. "Constructing Serious Violence and Its Victims: Processing a Domestic Violence Restraining Order." In *Social Problems in Everyday Life: Studies of Social Problems Work*, edited by Gale Miller, and James A. Holstein, 191–218. Greenwich, CT: JAI Press.

Ewick, Patricia, and Susan S. Silbey. 1995. "Subversive Stories and Hegemonic Tales: Toward a Sociology of Narrative." *Law and Society Review* 29: 197–226.

Fine, Gary A. 2002. "The Storied Group: Social Movements as 'Bundles of Narratives." In *Stories of Change: Narratives and Social Movements*, edited by Joseph E. Davis, 229–246. Albany, NY: State University of New York Press.

Fisher, Walter R. 1984. "Narration as a Human Communication Paradigm: The Case of Public Moral Argument." *Communication Monographs* 51: 1–22.

Fleury-Steiner, Benjamin. 2002. "Narratives of the Death Sentence: Toward a Theory of Legal Narrativity." *Law and Society Review* 36: 549–576.

Flopp, Leti. 2002. "The Citizen and the Terrorist." *UCLA Law Review* 49: 1575–1600.

Frank, Arthur W. 1995. *The Wounded Storyteller: Body, Illness, and Ethics*. Chicago, IL: University of Chicago Press.

Frank, Lauren B., Sheila T. Murphy, Joyce S. Chatterjee, Meghan B. Moran, and Lourdes Baezconde-Garbanati. 2015. "Telling Stories, Saving Lives: Creating Narrative Health Messages." *Health Communication* 30: 154–163.

Frye, Northrop. 1957. *Anatomy of Criticism*. Princeton, NJ: Princeton University Press.

Garro, Linda. 1994. "Narrative Representations of Chronic Illness Experience: Cultural Models of Illness, Mind, and Body in Stories Concerning the Temporamandibular Joint (TMJ)." *Social Science and Medicine* 38: 775–788.

Geertz, Clifford. 1973. *The Interpretation of Cultures*. New York, NY: Basic Books.

Gergen, Kenneth J. 1994. *Realities and Relationships: Soundings in Social Construction*. Cambridge, MA: Harvard University Press.

Gordon, Steven L. 1990. "Social Structural Effects on Emotions." In *Research Agendas in the Sociology of Emotions*, edited by Theodore D. Kemper, 134–179. Albany, NY: State University of New York Press.

Green, Brenda. 2013. "Narrative Inquiry and Nursing Research." *Qualitative Research Journal* 13: 62–71.

Gubrium, Jaber F., and James A. Holstein. 1997. *The New Language of Qualitative Method*. New York, NY: Oxford University Press.

Gubrium, Jaber F., and James A. Holstein. 2009. *Analyzing Narrative Reality*. Thousand Oaks, CA: SAGE.

Gupta, Kuhika, Joseph Ripberger, and Wesley Wehde. 2018. "Advocacy Group Messaging on Social Media: Using the Narrative Policy Framework to Study Twitter Messages about Nuclear Energy Policy in the United States." *The Policy Studies Journal* 46: 118–135.

Gusfield, Joseph. 1990. "Two Genres of Sociology: A Literary Analysis of the American Occupational Structure and Tally's Corner." *Sociological Methodology* 39: 1–29.

Hall, Stuart. 1980. "Encoding/Decoding." In *Culture, Media, Language*, edited by Stuart Hall, 128–138. London: Hutchinson.

Harvey, Mary R., Elliot G. Mishler, Karestan Koenen, and Patricia A. Harney. 2000. "In the Aftermath of Sexual Abuse: Making and Remaking Meaning in Narratives of Trauma and Recovery." *Narrative Inquiry* 10: 291–311.

Hasford, Julian. 2016. "Dominant Cultural Narratives, Racism, and Resistance in the Workplace: A Study of the Experiences of Young Black Canadians." *American Journal of Community Psychology* 57: 158–170.

Hochschild, Arlie R. 1979. "Emotion Work, Feeling Rules, and Social Structure." *American Journal of Sociology* 85: 551–575.

Holstein, James A., and Jaber F. Gubrium. 2000. *The Self We Live By: Narrative Identity in a Postmodern World*. New York, NY: Oxford University Press.

Holstein, James A., and Jaber F. Gubrium (eds). 2012. *Varieties of Narrative Analysis*. Thousand Oaks, CA: SAGE.

Holstein, James A., and Gale Miller. 1990. "Rethinking Victimization: An Interactional Approach to Victimology." *Symbolic Interaction* 12: 102–122.

Hutcheson, John, David Domke, Andre Billeaudeaux, and Philip Garland. 2004. "U.S. National Identity, Political Elites, and a Patriotic Press Following September 11." *Political Communication* 21: 27–50.

Imada, Toshie. 2012. "Cultural Narratives of Individualism and Collectivism: A Content Analysis of Textbook Stories in the United States and Japan." *Journal of Cross-Cultural Psychology* 43: 576–591.

Ingram, Mrill, Helen Ingram, and Raul Lejano. 2014. "What's the Story? Creating and Sustaining Environmental Networks." *Environmental Politics*, 23(6): 984–1002.

Järvinen, Margaretha, and Ditte Anderson. 2009. "The Making of the Chronic Addict." *Substance Use & Misuse* 44: 865–885.

Jasper, James. 1997. *The Art of Moral Protest: Culture, Biography, and Creativity in Social Movements*. Chicago, IL: University of Chicago Press.

Johannessen, Lars E.F. 2014. "Narratives and Gatekeeping: Making Sense of Triage Nurses' Practice." *Sociology of Health & Illness* 40: 892–906.

Jonsson, Rickard. 2014. "Boy's Anti-School Culture? Narratives and School Practices." *Anthropology and Education Quarterly* 45: 276–292.

Kavoori, Anandam P. 1999. "Discursive Texts, Reflexive Audiences: Global Trends in Television News Texts and Audience Reception." *Journal of Broadcasting & Electronic Media* 43: 386–398.

Kazyak, Emily. 2011. "Disrupting Cultural Selves: Constructing Gay and Lesbian Identities in Rural Locales." *Qualitative Sociology* 34: 561–581.

Keeton, Robert M. 2015. "'The Race of Pale Men Should Increase and Multiply': Religious Narratives and Indian Removal." In *Narrative Criminology: Understanding Stories of Crime*, edited by Lois Presser, and Sveinung Sandberg, 125–149. New York, NY: New York University Press.

Kirkman, M. 1998. "Adolescent Sex and the Romantic Narrative: Why Some Young Heterosexuals Use Condoms to Prevent Pregnancy But Not Disease." *Psychology, Health & Medicine* 3: 355–371.

Klapp, Orin. 1954. "Heroes, Villains, and Fools as Agents of Social Control." *American Sociological Review* 19: 56–62.

Klein, Kate, Alix Holtby, Katie Cook, and Robb Travers. 2015. "Complicating the Coming Out Narrative: Becoming Oneself in a Heterosexist and Cissexist World." *Journal of Homosexuality* 62(3): 297–326.

Kuroiwa, Yoko, and Maykel Verkuyten. 2008. "Narratives and the Constitution of a Common Identity: The Karen of Burma." *Identities: Global Studies in Culture and Power* 15: 391–412.

Laceulle, Hanne, and Jan Baars. 2014. "Self-Realization and Cultural Narratives About Later Life." *Journal of Aging Studies* 31: 34–44.

Lambek, Michael, and Jacqueline S. Solway. 2001. "Just Anger: Scenarios of Indignation in Botswana and Madagascar." *Ethnos* 77: 49–72.

Lauby, Fanny. 2016. "Leaving the 'Perfect DREAMer' Behind? Narratives and Mobilization in Immigration Reform." *Social Movement Studies* 15: 374–387.

Levinger, Matthew. 2018. "Master Narratives of Disinformation Campaigns." *Journal of International Affairs* 71: 125+.

Linde, Charlotte. 1993. *Life Stories: The Creation of Coherence.* New York, NY: Oxford University Press.

Linde, Charlotte. 2010. "Social Issues in the Understanding of Narrative." Papers from the Association for the Advancement of Artificial Intelligence. Fall Symposium. Association for the Advancement of Artificial Intelligence.

Lock, Andy, and Tom Strong. 2010. *Social Constructionism: Sources and Stirrings in Theory and Practice.* Cambridge: Cambridge University Press.

Loseke, Donileen R. 2003. *Thinking About Social Problems: An Introduction to Constructionist Perspectives*, 2nd ed. Piscataway, NJ: Transaction.

Loseke, Donileen R. 2009. "Examining Emotion as Discourse: Emotion Codes and Presidential Speeches Justifying War." *The Sociological Quarterly* 50: 499–526.

Loseke, Donileen R. 2012. "The Empirical Analysis of Formula Stories." In *Varieties of Narrative Analysis*, edited by James A. Holstein, and Jaber F. Gubrium, 251–272. Thousand Oaks, CA: SAGE.

Loseke, Donileen R. 2017. *Methodological Thinking: Basic Principles of Social Research Design*, 2nd ed. Thousand Oaks, CA: SAGE.

Loseke, Donileen R. 2019. *Narrative Productions of Meanings: Exploring the Work of Stories in Social Life.* Lanham, MD: Lexington.

Loseke, Donileen R., and Kirsten Fawcett. 1995. "Appealing Appeals: Constructing Moral Worthiness, 1912–1917." *The Sociological Quarterly* 36: 61–78.

Marvasti, Amir B. 2002. "Constructing the Service-Worthy Homeless through Narrative Editing." *Journal of Contemporary Ethnography* 31: 615–651.

McQueen, Amy, Matthew W. Kreuter, Bindu Kalesan, and Kassandra I. Alcaraz. 2011. "Understanding Narrative Effects: The Impact of Breast Cancer Survivor Stories on Message Processing, Attitudes, and Beliefs Among African American Women." *Health Psychology* 30: 674–682.

Merry, Melissa K. 2018. "Narrative Strategies in the Gun Policy Debate: Exploring Proximity and Social Construction." *Policy Studies Journal* 46: 746–770.

Morrell, Calvin, Christine Yalda, Madelaine Adelman, Michael Musheno, and Cindy Bejarano. 2000. "Telling Tales in School: Youth Culture and Conflict Narratives." *Law & Society Review* 34: 521–565.

Nolan, James L. Jr. 2002. "Drug Court Stories: Transforming American Jurisprudence." In *Stories of Change: Narrative and Social Movements*, edited by Joseph E. Davis, 149–178. Albany, NY: State University of New York Press.